QUIETLY RESTING

QUIETLY RESTING

Aletha Hinthorn

Beacon Hill Press of Kansas City
Kansas City, Missouri

Copyright 1996
by Beacon Hill Press of Kansas City

ISBN 083-411-6073

Printed in the
United States of America

Cover Design: Paul Franitza
Cover Photo: Index Stock

Library of Congress Cataloging-in-Publication Data
Hinthorn, Aletha.
    Quietly resting / Aletha Hinthorn.
       p. cm. — (Satisfied heart series)
    Includes bibliographical references.
    ISBN 0-8341-1607-3 (pbk.)
    1. Trust in God—Study and teaching. 2. Rest—Religious aspects—Christianity—Study and teaching. 3. Obedience—Religious aspects—Christianity—Study and teaching. 4. Peace of mind—Religious aspects—Christianity—Study and teaching. I. Title. II. Series: Hinthorn, Aletha. Satisfied heart series.
BV4637.H56 1996   96-5636
248.4—dc20   CIP

10   9   8   7   6   5   4   3   2   1

Contents

1

EXPLORING THE LAND OF REST

How little I believed the rest and peace of heart I now enjoy were possible down here! It is heaven begun below.[1]

—Hudson Taylor

Introduction

When I was a little girl, the well that supplied our house with water frequently went dry, so my dad decided to have a new well dug. He prayed about the exact location of our new well, and when the well drillers arrived, he announced that they were to drill about 30 feet east of our kitchen door.

After several days of digging, the well drillers struck water. "It's an artesian well!" they excitedly announced. The drillers packed up their equipment and left, but I hung around. "What is an artesian well?" I wondered.

For about an hour I kept running back to look at the pipe the drillers had left sticking out of the ground. Finally my attentiveness was rewarded. Clear, pure water began to flow out of the pipe. I sat there wide-eyed as the water overflowed like a fountain.

From that day on, a shortage of water was no longer a problem in our home. Even in the long summer months when others' wells were going dry, we had water.

It is this kind of spiritual well—an overflowing love, joy, and peace that keeps on flowing no matter the circumstances—that the Lord promises those who dwell in Him. The Spirit-filled life is to be a spiritual artesian well. As long as we allow His life to flow through us by continually trusting and obeying, we will experience a quiet rest and an overflow of the fruit of the Spirit.

When we're not dwelling in Christ, we may be able to be long-suffering and patient—but with joyfulness? The lavish outpouring of the Spirit into our hearts will cause us to overflow with joy, with the grace of giving, with good works, with hope, and with love. Jesus said, "Indeed, the water I give him will become in him a spring of water welling up to eternal life"; and "Streams of living water will flow from within him" (John 4:14; 7:38).

Discussion and Questions

The land of rest is a land of abundance. God shows the possibility of a victorious spiritual life by letting us picture the land of Canaan—the land of rest where the Israelites would lack nothing and where they could experience continual victory.

"The LORD said to Moses, 'Send some men to explore the land of Canaan, which I am giving to the Israelites'" (Num. 13:1-2). In this chapter we will explore the land of promise.

Why explore this land? "The promise of entering his rest still stands" (Heb. 4:1). Every promise given to the Israelites about their land of rest was significant, because each promise pictures similar possibilities for those who find rest in Christ. In our exploration we will look at only a few of those promises.

Moses briefly described this good land in Deut. 8:7-10. Let's examine carefully each of the descriptive terms used to describe Canaan and think of these expressions as portrayals of the kind of spiritual life we can have in Christ.

◆ You Will Lack Nothing!

1. The Israelites would experience no drought, because the land of Canaan was well-watered. What a pleasing description this was to those who had wandered nearly 40 years in a dry and parched desert!

Write the description of their water supply that is given in Deut. 8:7. Notice that they would have a water supply that totally met every need.

2. What do you think the promise of water represents? Consider John 4:13-14 and 7:37-39. What spiritual thirsts do we have that the Holy Spirit quenches?

"Do not change the Savior's words," Hudson Taylor often said. "It is not 'Whosoever has drunk,' but 'Whosoever drinketh.' The continuous habit of drinking prevents our ever thirsting again."

"Shall never thirst" (4:14, KJV)—would that prove true when Mr. Taylor's dear wife died and he lay sick? Would he really find that God supplied every unsatisfied need?

"How lonesome were the weary hours when confined to my room!" he wrote. "How I missed my dear wife! Then I understood why the Lord had made that passage so real to me, 'Whosoever drinketh of the water that I shall give him shall never thirst.' Twenty times a day, perhaps, as I felt the heart-thirst coming back, I cried to Him, 'Lord, You promised! You promised me that I should never thirst.'

"And whether I called day or night, how quickly He came and satisfied my sorrowing heart!"[2]

3. List the variety of foods found in Canaan, as listed in Deut. 8:8.

✎   wheat, barley, vines, fig trees, etc.

4. Read an almost identical list in Joel 1:11-12. According to these verses in Joel, what is gone when these foods are gone?

✎   joy is gone

5. How does the promise of joy relate to the spiritual life? Look at the following New Testament references:

✎   Acts 2:28

fill us w/ joy

✎   Rom. 14:17

peace

6. How richly supplied the Israelites would be in this new land! God not only gave them the basics (such as wheat and barley), but He also prepared special delights for them. Pomegranates were used to make cool, refreshing drinks, much as lemons are used today. How does that translate into the variety of blessings God provides for us? Consider 1 Tim. 6:17.

7. In Deut. 8:9 the Israelites were promised an abundance of bread. Who does "bread" represent? See John 6:35. What does bread provide for us spiritually?

8. The phrase "a land where the rocks are iron" (Deut. 8:9) implies that what would make others stumble could be a source of strength to them. Their land of rest would not be a land where all difficulties would be removed. Why might iron-containing rocks be better than the promise to have all rocks removed? How might the Holy Spirit use difficulties to help us?

9. The Israelites would also find that obstacles to climb wouldn't merely wear them down but would also be a source of riches. The difficult territory would yield rich benefits. (Copper was used in spears, balances, arms, vases, mirrors, statues, and cooking utensils.) The material for practical things that they used in their daily lives was pro-

vided. How does the Holy Spirit provide practical help for our daily lives?

◆ You Will Have an Overflow!

The language applied to the land of Canaan is now applied to our dwelling in Christ. This should not be surprising, since all that Canaan symbolized may now be experienced in Christ. Such words as "promise," "blessing," "rest," "dwelling," "fruit," "abundance," "riches," "peace," and "joy" can be used interchangeably to describe either dwelling in the physical land of Canaan or abiding in Christ.

The most frequently repeated description of Canaan was that it was "a land flowing with milk and honey." (The term is used 20 times, as in Deut. 6:3; 11:9; 26:9; and 26:15.) The Hebrew word "flow" meant "to flow freely," "to gush," "to overflow."

1. The word for "milk" meant "richness." What do you think honey represents? What did it provide in 1 Sam. 14:27?

Just as God promised the Israelites a superabundance of the very best (Deut. 28:11), God's provisions for us who dwell in Christ exceed all we can imagine. He enables us to live a victorious life through the power of the Holy Spirit. The Holy Spirit promises to provide richly for our every need until we not only have sufficient grace, but also an overflow of it.

Words such as "abundantly," "abounding," and "exceeding" are New Testament words used to describe the joy and grace we receive when the Holy Spirit abides within. The results of abiding in Christ will be infinitely better than we can imagine. "I am come that they might have life, and that they might have it more abundantly" (John 10:10, KJV).

His indwelling means our overflowing. Let's look at some of the areas in which we have been promised an overflowing abundance.

a. We will overflow in love. Fortunately, we don't have to draw upon our own supply of love. Use Rom. 5:5 and 1 John 3:1 to describe the measure of love God gives us.

As I sat at a friend's house, the restlessness in my spirit grew. Was I wasting my time? I had chosen to attend this affair out of love for my friend, but maybe I should have skipped the celebration. As I sat there harshly judging myself for not being at home working, I suddenly sensed God's pleasure. He knew I had come because I wanted to please Him by honoring my friend, and He was delighted that I had considered Him when I planned my schedule. As an awareness of His love filled me, I overflowed with a desire to show love to those around me.

See 1 Thess. 3:12. What are some of the ways you think Paul expressed his overflowing love?

What will be evidences in our lives that we overflow with love for others?

b. We will overflow in joy. Paul wrote, "In all our troubles my joy knows no bounds" (2 Cor. 7:4). Read 2 Cor. 8:2. Why does the joy of the Holy Spirit not depend upon favorable circumstances?

c. We will overflow in hope. The Greek word for "overflow," used in Rom. 15:13, means to "superabound" or be in excess. What attitudes would such hope eliminate?

d. We will overflow in fruit. Just as the Israelites were promised an abundance of fruit in the Promised Land (Deut. 28:11), we also are assured of bearing much fruit. When the Holy Spirit dwells in us, His life flows through us and overflows onto others. "Streams of living water will flow from within him" (John 7:38). Fruit, flavored by the Holy Spirit, results from that overflow. Name at least two things we learn in John 15:5, 8, and 16 about the fruit produced by the Spirit-filled life.

What will be the fruit we produce? For instance, see Gal. 5:22.

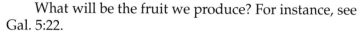

e. We will overflow in comfort. "Through Christ our comfort overflows" (2 Cor. 1:5). The Holy Spirit comes as our Counselor and Comforter. See John 14:16.

Deuteronomy 28:65-66 gives a picture of the heart not comforted. List at least four characteristics of this lack of rest.

f. We will overflow in power. In Eph. 3:20 we find the same Greek word applied to our experiencing and expressing His power. Because of the Holy Spirit's "power that is at work within us," He "is able to [carry out His purpose and] do superabundantly, far over and above all that we [dare] ask or think—infinitely beyond our highest prayers, desires, thoughts, hopes or dreams" (AMP.). It is our responsibility to let His power work unhindered through our thinking and actions.

Acts 1:8 tells us we'll receive power when the Holy Spirit comes upon us. What kinds of inner enemies will the Holy Spirit empower us to overcome?

g. We will overflow in praise and thanksgiving. What words or phrases in Eph. 5:20 and 1 Thess. 5:18 speak of abundant praise?

The Holy Spirit within us is a spirit of praise. At times, to refuse to praise God is to "quench . . . the Spirit" as 1 Thess. 5:19 warns against. One day while I was praying for God to supply the needs of a ministry I was involved with, I asked for the mind of Christ so I would know exactly how to pray. Immediately I was filled with a spirit of praise. How far behind I was in giving thanks for help He had already given! As I praised Him for His past help, I was filled with confidence that He would also provide for the future.

h. We will overflow in the grace of giving. Read 2 Cor. 8:1-2, 7. Giving is a grace, and the Holy Spirit, if unhindered, will plant within our hearts a desire to give. He invites us to be cheerful givers. The Greek word for "cheerful" is *hilaros*, from which we get the word "hilarious." How does this kind of giving differ from the natural way of giving?

i. We will overflow in good works. Notice that the promise of the Holy Spirit in 2 Cor. 9:8 uses the word "abound" twice. God is able to make us multiplied channels of blessing when we permit Him to infill and overflow us. What are the instructions and the promise in 1 Cor. 15:58?

Canaan, the land of abundance, was the land of rest. Hebrews 4:1 confirms that "the promise of entering his rest still stands."

The writer of Hebrews said, "They [those who disobeyed] were not able to enter, because of their unbelief" (3:19); but, "we who have believed enter that rest" (4:3).

Scriptural Role Model

When God first spoke to Abraham of the Promised Land, Abraham and his family lived in Ur, a place whose name meant "region of light." God gave Abraham's family enough light to see clearly to move to more satisfactory land.

Terah took his family, including his son Abraham, and set out for Canaan. "But when they came to Haran, they settled there" (Gen. 11:31). "Haran" means "parched."

Could this be a picture of many Christians? They've started for the Promised Land, the land where all their needs could be abundantly satisfied, but they're dwelling in Haran—a parched, dry land that lacks the abundance they could have if they moved on to Canaan.

Memorize

"Those who hope in me will not be disappointed" (Isa. 49:23).

Prayer

Dear Lord, I long for an overflow. How weary I am of having barely enough grace! I come to You empty. Please send me away full—even overflowing.

Thank You for lavishing grace, mercy, and love upon me. When You richly supply all my needs, I am more than satisfied. Let me be a channel of Your rich blessings to others. In Jesus' name I pray. Amen.

2

SURRENDER—THE ENTRANCE INTO REST

I remember the turmoil of soul I experi-
enced before committing myself to follow
Him on whatever path He would lead—re-
member as if it were yesterday. But at
last—oh, the rest that came to me when
I lifted my head and followed! *For in*
acceptance there lies peace.[1]

—Amy Carmichael

Introduction

The land of rest that we explored in the first chapter is not
entered casually. As we truly desire to dwell in this land of
abundance, the Holy Spirit will teach us how to rest in
Him. Sometimes His lessons are not easy.

I had been invited to speak at a women's retreat, and
after much preparation I arrived at the conference center,
excited to share what the Lord had given me. The first
night, after I was introduced, I arose to speak and dropped
the pen I had in my hand. I knew I should leave it on the
floor but bent to pick it up anyway—and when I did, my
pages of notes slid off the podium. This time there was no
choice, so once again the women saw me diving down, this
time to retrieve the notes under the table. Fortunately the
notes landed in a stack, but I'm certain that by this point

the women were fully awake, wondering just what might happen next to this unfortunate speaker.

That night as I got ready for bed, my spirit was not at rest. The next day as I spoke, I still felt the sting of embarrassment at such an awkward start. Although I sensed the Holy Spirit was at work, I felt like a failure.

I finished speaking, and as I sat down the Holy Spirit whispered, "You want to be thought of as a good speaker, don't you?" His tone was gentle, not chiding, as He tenderly revealed to me the source of my unrest. Earlier thoughts flashed through my mind. I recalled my admiration of good speakers and my hopes that others would give me that same praise.

"Would you be willing to continue speaking for Me even if you always feel like a failure when you finish?"

The cost of saying "yes" was painful. I pictured myself going to more retreats and feeling awkward, and I wanted to say, "No, please, Lord—I'd rather stay home." But I wanted His approval more than I wanted the comfort of knowing there would be no more embarrassing speaking situations. There was only one answer to give. During the concluding activities I sat on the front row with tears rolling down my cheeks, as my heart yielded to Him the role of defining what success would mean for me.

It is essential for us to know that the word "Canaan" means "to bend the knee" or "to humiliate," and that before the Israelites arrived in Canaan, they had to cross the Jordan River, a name that meant "to descend; to bring down; to subdue."

Songwriter Fanny Crosby summed up our dwelling in Canaan perfectly when she wrote, "Perfect submission, all is at rest." Not having any will of our own except a longing for His will to be fulfilled—that is perfect submission, and that is rest. "My meat [that which satisfies me] is to do the will of him that sent me" (John 4:34, KJV). That is the language of the satisfied heart.

Discussion and Questions

The heart not at rest is the heart troubled by desires that are not Christlike. To be able to surrender these desires to Him, we must first allow Him to show us what needs to be surrendered. We can't surrender what we don't realize is *un*surrendered. Second, we then offer ourselves to His lordship because we love Him. Finally, God responds to our love by purifying us of all that causes unrest.

◆ Discovering the Unsurrendered Self

Often our hindrance in surrendering is a lack of understanding what God requires of us. Being fully surrendered to God is so much more than obeying the Law, as the rich young ruler learned.

1. What did Jesus reply to the rich young ruler who asked which commands he should obey? See Matt. 19:17-19.

2. The young man was so pleased to say, "All these I have kept. . . . What do I still lack?" (Matt. 19:20). He was quite sure he had surrendered to all of God's commands. What did Jesus reply? See verse 21.

3. Jesus' words in verse 21 were not so much adding another command as they were a test to see if the young man had kept the spirit of the Law. It was as if Jesus said, "If you truly love your neighbor as yourself, as you say you do, then sell your possessions and give them to your neighbor."

Why was this a reasonable request to make of one who had boasted that he loved his neighbor as he loved himself?

4. Jesus said that if the young man sold everything, and gave the money to the poor, and followed Him, he would be perfect. Evidently Jesus saw that until the young man would willingly forsake his riches, he would be unable to love God wholeheartedly. Why do you think God does not need to require the same of everyone?

The Holy Spirit knows how to identify the points that are the most difficult for us to surrender to Him, those indications that we love something or someone else more than we love Him.

5. God always asks us to surrender what we would be tempted to hold between Him and ourselves. How little we know of our own hearts until the Holy Spirit reveals to us what is really there! Only He knows what a total surrender would mean to us. How do the following verses reveal that God is aware of hearts not completely surrendered to Him?

 1 Kings 15:3-5

 Matt. 23:5-7

 Acts 8:21

 Rev. 3:1

◆ Surrender Because You Love

1. Compulsory surrender is the result of force. Voluntary surrender is the result of love. Notice how important Abraham's love for God was in his surrender. See Gen. 22:16-18.

2. The Spirit seeks to find those whose hearts are perfect in love. Jesus does not want His followers to be swept away by a moment of emotion that quickly blazes and just as quickly dies. What was Peter's call to follow the Lord in John 21:15-17?

3. The question Jesus asked Peter is still the question He asks us. He's not asking, "Do you understand and believe all the theology taught at your church?" but "Do you love Me?" Our call to follow comes as a call to love. How did God express His yearning to have a people who love Him? See Deut. 5:29.

"Israel is reminded that what is needed on their part is not emotion, but devotion."[2] God wants hearts that will love and obey Him.

4. Notice the results of such love as described in Deut. 5:29.

5. Why does our desire to obey God affect the spiritual responses of the next generation?

◆ Conquering the Unsurrendered Self

The surrendered life is a life of rest, joy, and peace. But it comes only after an inward relinquishment to God's perfect will. Our selfish ambitions and desires to please ourselves must be offered to God as a sacrifice.

1. Why do you think God requires us to surrender our desires before we can know His will?

2. What command was given to the Israelites when God told them to take possession of Canaan, their Promised Land of rest? See Deut. 7:1-2.

"There remains, then, a Sabbath-rest for the people of God" (Heb. 4:9). Since the promise of rest remains, we too have a territory to take. The territory each of us is to take so we can possess the Sabbath-rest is our individual heart. God's instructions about how the Israelites were to conquer Canaan gives us insight into how to conquer our inner enemies.

3. Deuteronomy 7:1 states that the Israelites were to allow God to drive out the inhabitants of those nations that were stronger and larger than they were. We too have enemies stronger than we are. What inner unrest did Paul speak of in Rom. 7:15?

Just as the Israelites were to let God drive out their enemies, we also must look to Him for deliverance from our inner enemies. If we try to conquer our own self-will, pride, unbelief—all that would keep us from our promised rest—we'll discover we're no match for our enemies.

4. God offers to purify us of all that would keep us from desiring to be yoked with Him. The biblical prayers for purity assume we cannot attain a pure heart simply through our own efforts. Write the key phrases from the following prayers. Who is the One who creates the clean heart?

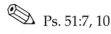 Ps. 51:7, 10

1 Thess. 5:23

Does He ask us to cleanse ourselves in 1 John 1:9?

"I don't think I've ever written anything 100 percent for the Lord—maybe 99 percent—but there's always at least some small selfish carnal pride in it," I once heard a writer confess.

The words of our great Purifier give wonderful hope: "He will sit as a refiner and purifier of silver; he will purify the Levites and refine them like gold and silver. Then the LORD will have men who will bring offerings in righteousness, . . . and the offerings . . . will be acceptable to the LORD" (Mal. 3:3-4).

"I will come and purify you of all your selfish motives," God promised through Malachi. "I will give you the ability to offer an offering that is totally acceptable to Me." After we have come before the great Purifier, it won't matter if our name doesn't appear on the article, if we're not selected as Sunday School teacher, if our name is overlooked at promotion time. It is not through our activities or the results of those activities, but it is our inner motivations that determine our ability to rest in Him.

What a rest comes when we're able to give offerings that are pleasing to God!

The picture of the Refiner in Malachi is one taken from Eastern life, in which the goldsmith sits on the floor by his crucible. Amy Carmichael told of visiting one of these Eastern goldsmiths and asking, "How do you know how long to sit and wait? How do you know when it is purified?"

"When I can see my face in it," he replied.

Our loving Refiner expects to see the reflection of His face even in our poor metal.[3]

Self-denial, which is the essence of surrender, does not necessarily mean giving up things; it means giving up self. The rich young man began at the right place. He asked Jesus what was required of him. We are to ask the Holy Spirit to reveal to us any unsurrendered territory. Then we must take time to allow Him to search our hearts, rather than do it ourselves. If we search our own hearts without direction from the Spirit, we might assume false guilt, or we might overlook our true needs.

5. In the time of surrender it's good to make a mental inventory of our lives—spirit, mind, body, strength, time, talents, character, reputation, possessions, relationships. Does He reveal to you that you love anything or anyone more than you love Him?

Rest is complete acquiescence to God's will. It's a perfect acceptance of whatever He allows to come. Have you surrendered your right to decide your attitudes, your successes, your ambitions?

6. Just as freely as God forgives us our sins, so He empowers us to love Him with all our hearts by purifying our hearts. What does Acts 15:8-9 say is our part?

7. Notice in Heb. 3:19 that believing God was what the Israelites failed to do. They doubted that God would really drive out their enemies, so they didn't enter the land of rest. Notice in 4:2-3, 9-10 how important faith is in our entering our promised rest.

In His rest, we find we have one desire—to delight Him. Once the Refiner has purified our heart from all that displeases Him, our joy is in giving Him pleasure. The heart at rest is a satisfied heart.

Scriptural Role Model

When Naomi and her two daughters-in-law decided to return to Naomi's home in Bethlehem, she knew they must fully realize the consequences of following her.

"Return home, my daughters. Why would you come with me? Am I going to have any more sons, who could become your husbands?" (Ruth 1:11), she asked Orpah and Ruth, her daughters-in-law. It was as though she said, "If your deepest desire is to have a husband, then forget following me."

Orpah, whose Hebrew name is taken from a word that means "stiff necked," wept as she said good-bye; but she recognized that following Naomi was not for her. She did want a husband more than she wanted to follow Naomi.

Ruth's Hebrew name meant "friend," and what a true friend she was! "Don't urge me to leave you or to turn back from you. Where you go I will go, and where you stay I will stay" (Ruth 1:16). Her deepest desire was to stay with Naomi and to follow her no matter the personal cost involved.

The assurance that Ruth truly wanted to be with her satisfied Naomi. "When Naomi realized that Ruth was determined to go with her, she stopped urging her" (Ruth 1:18).

We don't know what happened to Orpah, but we do know about the blessings Ruth received. She not only married Boaz, but her name is included in the genealogy of Jesus.

Jesus, too, is seeking those whose hearts love Him perfectly. Those who follow Him most closely will be those who have looked at the alternatives, have faced their tendencies to turn aside, and have renounced them. Then Jesus will be satisfied that their hearts are fully set on Him.

Memorize

"Test me, O LORD, and try me, examine my heart and my mind; for your love is ever before me" (Ps. 26:2-3).

Prayer

Dear Lord, I long to love You with all my heart. Cleanse me from all desires that would hinder me from loving You with a pure love.

I want to be entirely given to You. All that I have and all that I am, both now and in the future, I offer to You. Everything is Yours, and I am content to rest in Your choices.

Lord Jesus, let this be a reality! Bring this consecration about in me and through me. You know my weaknesses. Please let me never draw back from the commitment of this moment.

Thank You for calling me to a quiet rest, a rest so complete that I enjoy perfect peace as I trust in You. In Jesus' wonderful name. Amen.

3

LIVE IN CHRIST— LIVE IN LOVE

Is this not the reason why so many of God's children make so little progress? They do not know that the life of Christ who died on the cross and now lives in heaven is truly their life.[1]

—*Andrew Murray*

Introduction

For a year and a half before I began writing this book, the Holy Spirit gave me a lesson in quietly resting. I had waited for a decision that would directly affect my life in major ways. During those months of waiting, I began to look forward to the changes that would occur when the months of waiting were over. More than that, though, I looked to the Lord. His will would be perfect no matter what the outcome would be.

One Monday morning I received the anticipated phone call. The answer was no. What I had hoped would happen would not occur.

As I hung up the phone, wondering if my spirit would fall after learning that these months of anticipation were answered with God's no, I suddenly was filled with overwhelming joy. I knew it was not my joy—it was *His* joy. My

29

daughter entered the room, and while telling her about the phone call, I was so overcome by joy that tears began to flow.

When an apology was offered a few days later, I could honestly say, "I'm not disappointed. I was hoping in God, not in you."

"Those who hope in me will not be disappointed" (Isa. 49:23). Yet even that ability to hope comes from the Lord. Those who quietly rest in Christ trust Him to supply not only that rest but the *ability* to rest. It would be foolish to think we can experience rest through our own strength.

Rosalind Goforth said a turning point in her spiritual life came when she realized "that Jesus Christ was actually and literally within me. . . . I saw at last the secret of victory—it was simply Jesus Christ himself—His own life lived out in the believer." Once she made that discovery, she said that, like "a tired, worn-out wanderer finding home at last, I just rested in Him."

Years later when a friend asked her if she could sum up the result of this discovery in her life, she replied, "Yes, it can be all summed up in one word, 'Resting.'"[2]

Discussion and Questions

For us, to live in Canaan is to live in Christ. We rest, not because there are no battles, but because we go in His strength. Canaan, the land of rest, was a land of conquest. Just as the Israelites could not have lived in their Promised Land without continually trusting God for victory, so we too must learn to rest "in Christ."

In this chapter we'll look at what it means to rest in Christ. We'll also consider the oneness of living in Christ and living in love.

◆ Live in Christ

One of our greatest needs is to realize that Jesus lives in us just as definitely and fully as He lived in Nazareth.

Then, as we begin to grasp that glorious truth, we can learn to let our spirits rest in His indwelling Spirit.

1. How can we learn to rest in Christ? First, we must recognize that the "Christ life" is the incarnation of Jesus himself in our own lives. Let's look at the promise of Christ to come to live within us. What was Jesus' final prayer for us in John 17:26?

2. Notice that Jesus repeatedly made statements concerning His indwelling us. Why do you think He repeated this concept? See John 14:20, 23; 17:21-23.

3. How is having Christ dwelling within different from having Him beside us, as when He was on earth? What advantages would there be?

4. Because He was leaving, we could have new benefits. What did He promise us in John 14:27 and 15:11? Also, what does 1 Cor. 2:16 say we have?

We can't give our joy and peace to our spouse or children. We may give them knowledge of how to have joy or peace, but to actually give them the joy we have, we would have to enter them and be a part of them. That is what Jesus promised. We wouldn't just have knowledge of Him; He would reside in us.

Jesus said He had to go away so He could come again—not as a man to walk beside us, but as a spirit to live within us. The Christ life is Christ reliving His life in us and enabling us to be and to do what, in our own strength, we could never accomplish.

5. What words describing who indwells us are used interchangeably in John 15:5, 7; Rom. 8:9-10; and 1 John 4:12, 16? Why can they be interchanged?

6. What symbols did Jesus use to describe our union with Him in John 15:1-7? List at least two ideas these figures give you about the significance of our union with Christ.

A vine has no independent life of its own. If we abide in Him, then we are to constantly look to Christ to think His thoughts in us, to fulfill His purposes in us, and to feel His emotions and affections as though they were our own.

7. Our responsibility is to receive Christ, abide in Him, and have Him transform us day after day. He asks that we recognize our dependence and receive all from

Him. Paul wrote a beautiful description of this in Gal.
3:27—"You . . . have clothed yourselves with Christ." What
will be some of the marks of those who are clothed with
Christ?

Some may naturally think, "Such a person who cares
only about pleasing God must be otherworldly. How can
that person hope to connect with people if all he or she
cares about is pleasing God?" While it may seem that focusing on God would make us insensitive to others, the
opposite actually occurs. When we open ourselves to
God's Spirit, we receive His sensitivities. Our sensitivity
and concern for others deepens rather than dissipates.

8. In Eph. 3:16-17, Paul prayed that the Ephesians
would have Christ formed in them through faith. We
might be tempted to think Christ is formed in us through
our good works. Why is faith the one thing that is necessary?

9. Until Christ is formed within us, we cannot live
holy lives. Can we truly live completely dependent upon
the Holy Spirit as Jesus did? Consider 1 John 2:6.

10. If you don't know that Christ through the Holy
Spirit lives within you, read Luke 11:13 and accept these
words as His personal promise to indwell you.

◆ Live in Love

1. To better grasp what it means to have Christ living in us, let's consider another phrase that appears to be used interchangeably. See 1 John 4:16.

2. What do you think it means to "live in love"?

3. What is the promise in John 15:7 to those who abide in Christ?

4. What is a similar promise in 1 John 3:21-22?

5. John 15:7 promises that those who abide in Christ can have whatever they ask from God. The similar promise in 1 John 3:21-22 is made to those who have confidence when they come into God's presence. Read verses 17-20 of 1 John 3. According to these verses, how do we gain confidence to come into God's presence?

6. If we love with actions and in truth, our heart will not condemn us, and that will allow us to come to Him with confidence. Because we approach God with confidence, we will receive from Him anything we ask. Notice that the promise is bracketed on both sides with the command to love. How is it stated the second time? See verse 23.

One morning my husband, who was out of town, called and asked me to deliver a message to his secretary. I thought about it once during the day, decided to wait until later, and that evening realized that I had failed to complete his request. Soon he would be calling, and what would I say? My usual anticipation of his call was dimmed by my failure to obey his request. Suddenly a verse I had been studying had new meaning: "We have confidence . . . because we obey his commands" (1 John 3:21-22).

John was speaking of having confidence in prayer. In order to go before the Lord confident that He will hear me, I need to obey His commands. The context for these verses leaves no doubt about which command He meant. It was the command to love each other. Only as we show love can we rest in the confidence that He will answer our prayers.

7. "Your attitude should be the same as that of Christ Jesus" (Phil. 2:5). Would others see any of the following attitudes in you—frequently or even occasionally? Consider how these attitudes cause us to lack confidence that He answers our prayers.

Impatience
Bitterness
Complaining
Despair
Intolerance
Unforgiveness
Criticalness

8. Others will notice whether our spirits are loving. How would you finish the following statements?

My family would say I often have a(n) _____
spirit.

The Holy Spirit would probably say I tend to have
a(n) _____ spirit.

I am most tempted to have a(n) _____ spirit.

9. Write down the names of at least two people you
have been with in the last 24 hours. What words do you
think they would use to describe your attitude? Would
these words describe Christ's attitude toward them?

When my mother was a young lady, she once made
some critical remarks to an older friend. The friend replied,
"If you can't say something nice about someone, then
don't say anything."

Mother took that message to heart. I grew up in an atmosphere of love, hearing remarks like, "Let's put the best
construction on that comment that we can," and "He probably didn't mean that remark the way it seemed." She
didn't just say those words—she believed them. She always overlooked a potential personal offense.

As a result, she lived in love. We children knew we
could call on Mother and have her pray, and her prayers
would be answered.

10. To abide in Christ means we live in His atmosphere. We live so that the atmosphere around us is love.
Do we live in love? Would this be a description of us by
ourselves, by others, by God?

11. If we live in love, what would be indications to others?

12. "Live a life of love, just as Christ loved us" (Eph. 5:2). That is an impossible command! It may be a great relief to you to read 1 John 4:7.

What does God require of us? Simply that we be channels of His love by guarding our thoughts and words and by saying and thinking only what we know is acceptable to Him. If we provide the right words and thoughts, He'll provide the love. Love does come from God. We don't have to manufacture it ourselves—as if we could! We have only to ask for the mind of Christ.

As we seek to have the thoughts of Christ, when our habits or attitudes make Him feel ill at ease we will sense His discomfort. We can choose to ignore His indications that He is uncomfortable, or we can choose to abide in Him.

Showing love doesn't have to be a cycle of desperate striving and failing. When tempted to speak sharply or be ill-tempered, we're to abide in Him and pray, "Dear Lord, if those hurtful words and those slights had been directed toward You, if You had been misunderstood as I have, what attitude would You have? Give me that mindset, the mind of Christ." He will give us His thoughts when we're ready to lay down our defenses and give up our right to be understood and treated with patience.

One morning I disagreed with someone. Although I wanted to state my disagreement, I could sense my words wouldn't be spoken in love, so I fled to my Refuge by silently praying, "You're my Refuge, Lord. I hide in You. I won't say a word You don't provide." I hid in my Refuge until the temptation passed.

13. Notice the difference love made in Paul's praying. See Phil. 1:6-8. Why do you think we can more easily believe God hears us if we love the one for whom we pray?

Have you ever tried praying for someone after criticizing him or her? It's like trying to ride a sled down a hill when there's no snow on the ground.

14. "Be clear minded and self-controlled so that you can pray. Above all, love each other deeply" (1 Pet. 4:7-8). I would have stated that verse differently. I would have said, "Above all, pray." Why do you think Peter ranked praying and loving in the order he did?

"Do everything in love," Paul wrote in 1 Cor. 16:14. What a perfect motto for our lives as we strive to live in Christ!

Scriptural Role Model

Sometimes we go about loving in the reverse order of what Jesus did. Jesus loved us "while we were yet sinners" (Rom. 5:8, KJV). We, however, tend to withhold our demonstrations of love when someone doesn't please us.

If we had been God, we would have first sent the Holy Spirit to convict the world of sin (John 16:7-11). Then when everyone was sufficiently repentant, we would have sent our son to die. But *while we were yet sinners*, Christ died for us.

If we want to be like Christ, we, too, will not wait until others are pleasing us to give them the deepest expression of our love.

Memorize

"The mind controlled by the Spirit is life and peace" (Rom. 8:6).

Prayer

Thank You, Lord, for the possibility of living in You. All I have to offer You is a willingness to let Your attitude be my attitude. Teach me to live in You continually, to live in love and then to have confidence in Your presence. May the words of my mouth, and the meditation of my heart, be acceptable in your sight, O Lord, my Strength and my Redeemer. In Jesus' name. Amen.

4

THOSE AT REST LEARN DEPENDENCE

To depend upon His strength must become my greatest rest.[1]

—*Julian of Norwich*

Introduction

"Now, children, move your arms in rhythm to the music," the teacher instructed a group of physically challenged children. Only one little girl could keep with the beat perfectly. What was her secret? The instructor was standing behind the girl and moving her arms. The girl, totally relaxed, allowed the instructor to choose every move.

I think this is the concept Paul had in mind when he wrote Gal. 5:25—"If we live then by the (Holy) Spirit, let us also walk by the Spirit—If by the (Holy) Spirit we have our life [in God], let us go forward walking in line, our conduct controlled by the Spirit" (AMP.).

We who have Christ in us are to allow Christ to relive His life through us. We are to walk in step with Him so we walk just as He walked when He was on earth. To keep in step with the Spirit, we allow the Spirit's gentle guidance to choose our every move.

The very fact that we can have our conduct controlled by the Spirit is astonishing. It's one of those facts about which we should "stand in awe" (Ps. 33:8, KJV).

Discussion and Questions

Our rest comes from yielding to the Holy Spirit's control. What are the secrets to this kind of restful dependence? Let's examine what our lives will look like when controlled by the Spirit.

◆ Resting from Our Own Works

The only way we can "enter God's rest" and live a restful, dependent life as Christ did is to rest from our own works. See Heb. 4:10.

1. To rest from our own works is to refrain from doing those things that are out of step with the Spirit. They are our works—not the will of God. These could include nagging, pouting, complaining, worrying—things we do when we are trying to make things happen our way, rather than trusting God to do His work in His way. Can you think of any "works" you do rather than relying upon the Holy Spirit?

2. Write the phrases from the following verses that show that Jesus ceased from His own works and lived only to please His Father.

 John 5:30

 John 7:16

3. If we are self-driven, if we set out on ventures, say words, or manipulate situations without the knowledge that we've been "sent" by God, what is accomplished? See John 6:63.

When we speak to others out of frustration instead of love; when we nag, prod, or push to have our way; when we try to manipulate situations to accomplish God's will—in short, when we are acting on our own—we need an alarm in our minds echoing the words of John 6:63. "The flesh counts for nothing. The flesh counts for nothing."

Usually our frustrated attitude says, "I will change you through force rather than faith." I have a little rhyme I say to myself when tempted to speak out of irritation rather than to wait on the Lord: "My words are like the sticks / of John 15:6." This verse speaks of the worthlessness of our deeds when we're not abiding in Christ. It states that such acts are like "branches . . . thrown into the fire and burned." They accomplish nothing beneficial.

If our confidence is in God, however, our attitude might be "I know God will help you," or "I'm listening to you." Then we can take in others' words, all the while listening to God for His instruction.

4. When we have learned to cease from our own works, the Holy Spirit's energy will work through us as it did through Christ. What could be indicators in your life that you are *not* depending upon the Spirit but are doing your own works?

5. "Here is my servant, whom I uphold," God said, speaking prophetically of Jesus in Isa. 42:1. Could God say the same about us? Would He say, "They are depending upon Me—they do only the work I enable them to do"?

If we think we can help someone in our own strength, we're failing to follow Christ's leadership. What did it mean for Jesus to be upheld by God?

6. Often we do see results when we forge ahead in our own strength. However, we soon discover that our own efforts are not lasting and in the end don't accomplish God's work. What did Jesus say about His abilities? Do we feel our dependence upon God as He did? Compare John 5:19 with John 15:5.

7. "Am I depending upon God?" That is the basic question. If I'm a Sunday School teacher, am I content when everyone seems to enjoy the class and we have a good discussion? Or am I unsatisfied unless I know I'm depending upon the Holy Spirit to teach? When I invite guests into my home, am I content with friendly chatter, or do I want to know that God is pleased with our conversation? What are some of the areas in your life in which you want to learn to depend upon the Holy Spirit?

8. What are some indicators you can begin to use as signals that you are depending upon yourself and not upon God? For instance, if we depend upon God, are we easily discouraged or upset if things don't go our way?

To rest quietly is to learn to lean upon the Lord, to rest in the knowledge that He is in control. Rest speaks of faith, of strong confidence that God has good purposes for all our efforts.

9. Why did the Israelites fail to cease from their own works and not enter the rest God wanted to give them? See Heb. 3:18-19.

10. Discuss why all our failures to let Christ live His life through us have the same origins as that of the Israelites—either unbelief or disobedience.

◆ Doing His Work

We can do more while resting than at any other time, because while we are resting from our own works, we enter His rest. See Heb. 4:10. Paul often spoke of his work as though Christ were doing it. When we realize how little we actually do when God does His work through us, we realize that our most profitable activity is to rest in Him.

1. What is God's role in our work, according to the following verses?

 Eph. 1:11

 Eph. 2:10

Phil. 2:13

Col. 1:29

Col. 4:17

2. In 2 Cor. 5:18-20, what does Paul say is our responsibility and what is God's?

3. Who ultimately brings people to believe in Christ? See John 16:7-11.

4. How do our attitudes differ when we are conscious that God makes His appeal through us, rather than when we feel that the results are up to us alone?

5. Although we depend upon the Holy Spirit to convict, God draws others to himself through human kindness. Read Hos. 11:4 in several versions. God will use our kindnesses as cords to draw others. Is there someone for whom you are praying? What acts of kindness could you do that God could use to draw that one to himself?

6. Although God uses our efforts, we are not to think that our efforts accomplish His work. Paul wrote a telling phrase to Timothy: "God's work—which is by faith" (1 Tim. 1:4). Discuss why our works are made effective by our faith.

7. In Rev. 1:20 Jesus stands in the midst of the candlesticks, or lampstands. The lampstands represent the Church. What is the role of a lampstand? How does that role differ from the role of light itself? How can this concept make us realize our dependence upon the Holy Spirit?

8. We are called to be holders of the light, not the light itself. Wouldn't the command be impossible to obey if we were the light rather than the light holders? How does that bolster our confidence in evangelizing?

9. Although we are not to think we can win others in our own strength, our efforts will accomplish great things if we trust in God. How effective did Jesus consider our words to be? See John 17:20.

10. As we abide in the Vine, we will produce fruit (John 15:5). It is as normal for Spirit-filled Christians to bear fruit as it is for a healthy apple tree to produce apples. A branch on an apple tree doesn't groan, "If only I could produce apples!" It *naturally* produces them. Neither does a branch removed from the tree produce fruit. Our fruit bearing depends on our union with Christ and on our responsiveness to the Holy Spirit.

Notice the fruit mentioned in Gal. 5:22-23 and consider the connection between winning souls and bearing the fruit of the Spirit.

11. God considers it a serious offense when we think we've done His work in our own strength. He told Gideon before he went to fight, "You have too many men." Why did God want Gideon to decrease his army size? See Judg. 7:2-3.

12. Sometimes God cannot use our efforts because He could not receive the glory from them. In what area of your life could God be hindered from accomplishing His purposes, because you seem to be able to do a decent job in your own strength?

13. Just because we do something well does not mean we are not depending upon God's empowerment. A better guide might be whether or not we frequently ask God to help us. What could be signs of self-effort in your life? Also, consider what might be some evidences that He is working through you.

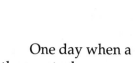

One day when a group of men were swimming, one of them got a leg cramp and was about to drown. A bystander called to one who was a good swimmer, but the swimmer hesitated and appeared to be unconcerned about the drowning man. Just before the sinking man would have drowned, the good swimmer in a few swift strokes reached the man and took him to safety.

Later someone chided the good swimmer for failing to respond more quickly. He replied, "You can never rescue a swimmer until he's completely exhausted his resources. If I had gone to him earlier, he would have pulled me down, and we both would have drowned."

God also often waits until we are ready to give up self-dependence and are willing to let Him do what He desires. If we don't sense His help, maybe He's delaying until we will not hinder His work by trying to do it our own way.

14. Often our problem is not so much that we're depending upon ourselves as it is that we're afraid to depend upon God. Read Judg. 6:15. What were Gideon's words?

15. What would enable Gideon to accomplish his mission? See verse 16.

16. Once God firmly convinced Gideon that He would "save Israel by [Gideon's] hand as [He had] promised" (6:36), then Gideon set himself to obey. God wants us to be fully confident that He is with us, will give us the victory, and will use what we do. Such confidence allows us to take risks others would fear to take. We can proceed, resting in the knowledge that He will provide all we need. We don't gain rest through our own efforts but through our confidence in God.

If we will depend upon God, He will give us evidence that He will enable us. What did God do for Gideon in Judg. 7:9-15?

17. I recently attended a planning session for a new ministry, and the leader opened with a confession: "When we began planning this ministry, I prayed hours for it. Lately, though, it has seemed that everything was going well, and I quit praying so much." She requested that we spend the first part of the meeting in prayer.

It's often easy to sense our need of God's help in the beginning of a new situation. When He helps us, however, we often tend to forget that without Him we can do nothing. What did God warn the Israelites about in Deut. 8:10-16?

18. Instead of giving God praise, what would the Israelites be tempted to do? See Deut. 8:17-18.

19. In verses 19 and 20, what did God say would be the result of their failing to give Him honor?

20. God's strength is made perfect not in our strength, but in our weakness. He doesn't say, "You're great. You can do it." What did He call Israel in Isa. 41:14?

21. Read verses 15 and 16. What can God do with a lowly "worm"? What "mountains" in your life could He take care of through you if you could only become small enough for Him to use?

Scriptural Role Model

A man came to his friend at night, begging for some bread. "A friend of mine on a journey has come to me, and I have nothing to set before him" (Luke 11:6). How often we would do well to recognize our needs! "It's time for devotions, Lord, and I have nothing to set before my family." "I'm going to visit an unsaved friend. I don't know what to say. I must have some bread to share." "My patience is exhausted. Fill me with Your love."

As we live with the Spirit of Jesus, who said, "I can do nothing . . ." (John 5:30) and look to Him with confidence, we'll discover rest—the rest that allows the Holy Spirit to provide richly all we need, because we've ceased from our own works.

Memorize
"Find rest, O my soul, in God alone; my hope comes from him" (Ps. 62:5).

Prayer

Dear Lord, You see that I am often hindered from enjoying the land of rest because I don't let go of self-effort. I think I am able to accomplish Your work through my might and my power. Help me to remember that I can do nothing except by Your Spirit. Thank You for being my loving Savior, who has offered to give me rest, and who promises to supply all my needs. In Jesus' name I pray. Amen.

5

DISCOVERING THE ENEMIES OF OUR REST

I learned that worship and worry cannot live in the same heart: they are mutually exclusive.[1]

—*Ruth Bell Graham*

Introduction

While attending a seminar, I began the first day with a sweet awareness of resting in the Lord. By that evening I was praying, "Lord, why did I lose that sense of resting in You as the day progressed?" I dreaded going back the second day without an inner confidence that I was abiding in Him.

The next morning as I drove to the meeting, I recalled these words of Paul: "I have been crucified with Christ and I no longer live, but Christ lives in me" (Gal. 2:20).

The Lord reminded me of some of the less than loving thoughts I had entertained the day before about some of the people I was with. He would not allow me to have those. He let me know that I was to crucify such thinking on a thought-by-thought basis if I wanted to rest in Him. I could not dwell in Him if I allowed critical, proud, or unkind thoughts.

Paul wrote, "We take captive every thought to make it obedient to Christ" (2 Cor. 10:5). W. B. Godbey taught that the Greek word for "captive" is a very strong word signifying complete captivity.[2] Paul recognized how prone our thoughts are to wander off and then be captured by the enemy, so he commanded us to pursue our thoughts as though we're soldiers in wartime. We're to overtake our thoughts and bring them back to the "obedience of Christ" before Satan takes them captive. If we do not conquer our thoughts, they will very likely force us out of the land of rest and bring us into bondage.

Discussion and Questions

We need to identify areas of unrest in our lives. To continue to find rest, we must come again and again to Christ. If we don't have rest, it is because we have not come to Him in our immediate situation.

Our need for rest varies according to our personality, background, current situation, and many other factors. Sometimes we fail to rest in the Lord because we haven't consciously brought an area of unrest to Him. Possibly we haven't realized it is an area in which we are leaning on our own strength.

In this chapter we'll consider specific areas in which the Lord will give us rest. Perhaps these ideas will stimulate you to allow the Lord to help you identify any other areas of unrest in your life. Notice how frequently we must take our thoughts captive if we're to dwell in Christ.

◆ A. *Do I rest in the Lord when I need appropriate words?*

1. For those who are timid or afraid they might say the wrong thing, God gives a wonderful word. See Prov. 10:32.

2. Why do you think this promise is limited to those who are righteous?

3. The righteous (in Prov. 10:32) are those whose motives are to please God with their words. List three things that will be true of the kinds of comments a righteous person makes.

4. List three kinds of comments a righteous person would not make.

5. Since the Holy Spirit does not give "a spirit of timidity" (2 Tim. 1:7), what could be some evidences that we are not resting in Him?

6. When we depend upon the Spirit for our words, He enables us to clothe our thoughts in words better than we could otherwise have chosen—yet our individuality is not destroyed.

How did both Jesus and Paul state that they did not trust in their own abilities to choose their words?

 John 8:28

 1 Cor. 2:13-14

Recently my husband and I were going to a banquet with some people he knew but I didn't. I recognized that I might not feel at ease in this situation. Before we left I had a few moments alone with the Lord. I prayed, "Father, I'm resting in You tonight. I'm trusting You to give me what I should say."

The evening was incredibly easy. Throughout the dinner I simply rested. Later I marveled as I recalled the appropriate comments that had seemed so natural to make. The evening left me with a greater confidence—not in myself, but in the One who said, "I will come to give rest" (Jer. 31:2).

◆ B. *Do I trust the Lord not only for my words but also for my thoughts?*

1. For us to abide in Christ is to look constantly to Him to think His thoughts in us, to fulfill His purposes in us, to feel His emotions and affections as though they are our own. What does 1 Cor. 2:16 say we have access to?

2. Are we willing to assume the mind of Christ in every situation? Are we willing to think as He would think and to accept whatever He chooses, trusting Him to be in control? What are some of Christ's attitudes that you want Him to live out through you?

When we have the Holy Spirit living within us, Jesus joins himself to us so closely, and with a communication so real, that every other union we know is but a shadow of our union with Christ. The result of our uniting with Christ, however, is not some sort of mystical union that doesn't allow us to have our individual identities. Actually, we are never more ourselves than when we are walking in the Spirit. God is delighted with the personality He placed within each of us, and He wants to express himself through the one He gave us.

3. Why is it we are often "not ourselves" when we have attitudes that displease the Holy Spirit?

"Give me the mind of Christ" is a prayer to pray when we recognize we're having trouble possessing a loving attitude, or when we lack wisdom.

Another prayer for those "in Christ" to pray is, "Help me to be Christ to others." When this is our request, we'll find ourselves loving, listening, and perhaps even giving financial or practical help.

◆ C. *Do I rest in the Lord when tempted to be afraid of violence?*

1. If we begin to focus on the many news reports of crime in our country, we might lose the peace the Lord wants us to enjoy. God encourages us to trust Him for His protection. Notice in Ps. 27:1-5 the psalmist's confidence in the protection of God.

2. "The LORD will fulfill his purpose for me" (Ps. 138:8). How does this encourage you to trust God to shield you so that He allows only what His purposes include?

A friend who lived in a dangerous area was having difficulty sleeping at night. One night when she was awakened by some noise and went to peer anxiously out the window, the Lord spoke to her about her fear: "Your fear is as much of Satan as of the gangs' activities." From that point on, she began to rest in the Lord, knowing that if He protected her family, they had nothing to fear.

3. Rather than fear the violent person, who does Matt. 10:28 tell us to fear? Why should this be our focus?

4. Discuss the differences between a healthy fear and a debilitating fear.

◆ **D.** *Do I tend to rest in the Lord only when things go as I expected and as I prefer?*

Those who rest in the Lord have the habit of accepting each thing that comes to them with the confidence that their loving Father is aware of it and will bring good through it. If we see God as always in control, determining the ultimate results, we can rest no matter what happens. Resting is believing that God has a good purpose—even if Satan might have initiated our troubles.

1. Notice that the psalmist does not imply that the righteous will never have trouble. Instead, what are they promised?

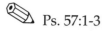 Ps. 34:19

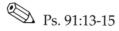 Ps. 57:1-3

 Ps. 91:13-15

 Ps. 94:19

 Ps. 145:14

2. Believing God brings good through every circumstance to all who trust in Him is quite different from saying that everything that happens is good. It is saying that in no situation can Satan cause all things to work together for evil. We can rest at all times, because we know the outcome will be good—as God defines good—for those who trust Him. What does the last phrase of Isa. 49:23 promise?

We want to encourage others to believe Rom. 8:28 when something bad happens to them, but for us to believe it when the tire is flat in the morning is a different story. Yet it is in the difficult situations that we need a resting place. When all flows smoothly, when we are treated well, when all our relationships are loving, are we as aware of resting in God? Our rest in Him is most precious when we have no one else to rest in. When all is gone but His faithfulness, we can know He shields us with His kindness.

My laser printer refused to work about midnight one Saturday when I was ready to print off the notes to use for teaching Sunday School the next morning. Did I fret? Not really. The Lord is in control of all that comes to me. I knew there might be several reasons God might allow this malfunction:

• Maybe the Lord wanted me to depend upon Him instead of the pages of notes. Teaching from a few handwritten notes rather than 10 typed pages might allow me to trust more fully in Him.

• I also recognized that, when such things occur, God probably has a higher plan than I could imagine. It's enough to know that "he guards the course of the just" (Prov. 2:8).

3. Write Rom. 8:28 in your own words, inserting a present situation from your own life in which you've been slow to believe this promise.

4. Now write three ways God could bring good from that situation.

 a.

b.

c.

God does not ask us to believe that a situation caused by our (or another's) sin is good. But as we look to Him and rest in Him, He will show His faithfulness to us.

Faith is the satisfied assurance that God will bring good through all that comes to us as we trust in Him. He will work things out in the future far better than we could work them out, so we rely on Him and trust Him in each situation.

It's amazing how the attitude that says, "God is in control—He will provide all I need," will carry us over rough spots and enable us to find rest in Him.

◆ E. *Do you rest in the Lord when you're busy?*

1. Often we find ourselves easily distracted when we have many jobs to do. Instead of resting in Him, we become upset by minor irritations and find that, rather than resting, we're stressed. Notice exactly what Jesus told Martha in Luke 10:41. Did He say she was *doing* too many things?

2. Being anxious and disturbed about too many things is not the same as *doing* too many things. What "one thing" do you think Jesus wanted Martha to do? See verse 42.

3. Mary had learned to focus on the Lord, to commune with Him. That is possible to do even when we are doing many things. What kinds of things help you to keep focused on Christ?

4. What kinds of things hinder you from focusing on Christ?

◆ F. *List at least one area of major concern in your life in which you would like to have rest.*

What can you do to find rest in this area? What verses could help you?

Scriptural Role Model

After Jesus warned Martha not to allow her many jobs to distract her from having Him as her single focus, we see her serving again in John 12:2. This time there is no mention of her complaining about her sister.

Her delight was now in serving others as she gave a meal in honor of her Lord. As she walked past Jesus, busily serving others, perhaps she caught His eye and saw that He was delighting in her serving others for Him. She was pleasing Him, and that knowledge filled her with contentment. Her eyes were now on Jesus—not on Mary.

It's when we focus on other people that we become troubled about many things. Only one thing is needed—a single focus on doing all we do for His glory. Jesus is saying, "In your busiest times, look to Me and see My pleasure in what you're doing. Find your delight in doing your work for Me." We find rest, when pleasing Him is our one desire.

Memorize

"Cast your cares on the LORD and he will sustain you; he will never let the righteous fall" (Ps. 55:22).

Prayer

Dear Lord, how thankful I am to find my rest in You in all parts of life! You allow me to rest in You when I need appropriate words. You even help me to have Your thoughts. In times of disappointment, I can know that Your love shields me, and that You will provide all I need. Enable me to take all my thoughts captive so that at all times I cast my cares on You. I pray this in Jesus' name. Amen.

6

INNER ATTENTIVENESS

Rest in God's love. The only work you are required now to do is to give your most intense attention to His still, small voice within.[1]

—Madame Jeanne Guyon

Introduction

Brother Lawrence served for 60 years as a cook to his fellow Carmelite monks in Paris, where he died in 1691. He endeavored constantly, as he put it, "to walk in His presence." Kitchen duty was not a job Brother Lawrence preferred. Despite this, he accepted his job humbly, and instead of focusing on his job, he learned to listen attentively to God.

He would enter his kitchen praying, "O my God, since Thou art with me, and I must now, in obedience to Thy commands, apply my mind to these outward things, I beseech Thee to grant me the grace to continue in Thy presence."

Notice that Brother Lawrence "practiced the presence" through God's enabling, not on his own. He asked God for "grace to continue."

God so abundantly answered his prayer that he later wrote, "The time of business does not with me differ from the time of prayer. And in the noise and clatter of my kitchen, while several persons are at the same time calling for different things, I possess God in as great tranquillity as if I were upon my knees at the blessed sacrament."[2]

Discussion and Questions

Our ability to rest in the Lord depends upon our ability to listen attentively. Let's consider the importance of listening, the results of listening, and finally look at some instructions for listening.

◆ Listening Is Not Optional

Joshua had just died, and the Israelites faced the first battle against the Canaanites without their leader. In Judg. 1:1 they asked the Lord which one of the tribes should be the first to go to battle. God replied that Judah should go first. The word "Judah" means "celebration" or "praise." Going forward in our battles with praise increases our awareness of our dependence upon God.

1. What invitation did the men of Judah give to the Simeonites? See Judg. 1:3.

2. The Hebrew word for "Simeon" meant "hearing." The root word meant "to hear intelligently," often implying hearing with attention and obedience. Praising isn't enough; we must also have a spirit of inner attentiveness— a spirit that is sensitive to the voice of the Holy Spirit. Both a spirit of praise and a listening spirit protect us from mistakes. These two attitudes are the most important in our maintaining a spirit of rest. Why are they both necessary?

3. How would being attentive to the Spirit encourage us to have a spirit of praise?

4. Jesus said He always obeyed the Father's promptings. If He needed to listen attentively, then certainly we do too. Notice what Jesus said about the words He spoke:

 John 8:28

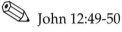 John 12:49-50

 John 14:10

John 17:8

5. Jesus prayed that we may also be one with the Father. Can we train ourselves to be constantly tuned to God's voice as Jesus was? Read John 14:10-12. What does Jesus say we will do if we have the Father in us? Also read John 16:15.

When the Holy Spirit prompts us, our response is always important. Sometimes we're tempted to think, "This

is a small matter. Ignoring the still, small voice won't matter this time." But the Spirit's leadings are always more important than we can realize at the time.

◆ Results of Listening

1. When we're listening to the Spirit we'll be perceptive and rational—not flighty, prejudiced, or dogmatic. We
will be calm and perceptive, like our inner Teacher. What
would you list as other results of listening?

God's plan is to give us rest so we can work for Him
with ease and success. There is no mistaking the one who
has found Christ's rest. That person has a poise of spirit
that cannot be counterfeited.

2. What are the results of wisdom listed in James 3:17-
18?

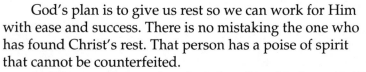

3. Which of these evidences of wisdom do you most
want to increase in your life? Why?

4. In Matt. 11:29-30, how does Jesus tell us to find
rest?

5. We are to learn from the One with whom we're yoked. We learn by looking to Him and asking, "What would You do in this situation? How would You respond to this, Lord?"

As we keep looking to Him to learn how we are to act, what kind of spirit do we see He always has, according to verse 29?

English writer William Law wrote, "When he says, 'Learn of me,' he does not say, 'for I am just and equitable, or kind, or holy,' but 'I am meek and lowly in heart'; as if he would teach us that these are the tempers which most of all distinguish his spirit."[3]

6. Jesus is saying, "Do you want rest? Then watch Me. I am always gentle and humble." How would understanding that a humble spirit gives us wisdom help us to know proper responses in many of life's situations? Can you think of a current relationship or situation in which you could show a humble attitude?

7. Why does a lack of humility cause unrest?

8. In the following verses from Matthew, how did Jesus show humility?

 8:20

 9:11

 15:1-3

 17:5-9

9. When any of the following statements are true, they may indicate a lack of humility. Consider how such an attitude leads to unrest in our spirits.

• I care more about others' opinions of me than about others' needs.

• I close people out of my life when I'm embarrassed to let them see me the way I am.

• I care more about what the people I label as "important" think, than what those I feel to be "unimportant" think.

• I take credit that belongs to God or to another.

If we're at rest, we let Him live through us. We look to Him, yield to His yoke, and seek to learn from Him how to have a gentle and humble spirit.

10. What are some attitudes we should recognize as being those of our own nature and not of Christ's?

When I began leading home Bible studies, I found one thing was essential if I was to depend upon the Spirit. I needed to pray until I was confident that the Lord would help. Then I taught with the assurance that the Spirit was directing my thoughts. When I failed to prepare myself through believing, I discovered I was looking for signs that those in the group had profited. If there were none, it was easy to become discouraged. However, when I trusted God to help I could leave the results with Him. The secret was to keep my focus on the Lord and not on the people.

One day one of the ladies said, "I guess you're becoming discouraged with us." I don't recall what I said, but I remember thinking, "Oh, no. I'm not looking at your progress—I'm looking to the Lord." I didn't become discouraged as long as my concern was "Am I trusting Him to lead?"

11. How does an inner looking to God protect us from burnout and stress?

◆ Learning to Listen

1. When the glory of the Lord appeared to Moses in the burning bush, he did the most important thing he

could have done. He said, "I will now turn aside, and see
. . ." (Exod. 3:3, KJV). God still seeks to reveal His glory to
us, but we too must turn aside to see. How can we communicate to the Lord that we want to turn aside to hear Him?
What are ways you can turn aside?

2. If we don't take time to hear Him when we're alone
with Him, we seldom hear Him at other times. Our ability
to hear God is best developed in our private devotions. It
was often at the time of worship that God spoke. For instance, see Gen. 12:6-9.

3. Why do we need to get quiet to hear God's voice?
How is God's voice described in 1 Kings 19:12?

4. Many who have wanted to hear God have learned
the value of using a notebook in their time of worship. An
open notebook beside us as we read the Bible can indicate
to God that we expect Him to speak. Often insights come
as we "turn aside to see" by writing down a verse that we
want to understand better.

Another use for a notebook is to write our prayers to
God and then record what we think He would say to us. If
we begin by asking God to give us His thoughts, such active listening is often rewarded with new insights and
strong assurances of His love for us.

Have you found other ways to hear God?

Active listening requires resting in Him, remembering that "we have the mind of Christ" (1 Cor. 2:16). As we take time to be in His presence, we learn it is through faith, a moment-by-moment trust, that we have His mind. He responds to our faith by giving us His thoughts, counsel, plans, and knowledge. We know His responses and His thoughts when we submit our will to Him and trust Him to give us His mind.

5. Write two reasons why faith is necessary to hear God.

After I had directed a business meeting, I wondered why I hadn't sensed God's direction. The next morning I read the account in Num. 16 about Moses' deciding what to do with Korah. At each point Moses prayed and waited until he knew what God wanted before he spoke to the people. "This was your trouble," the Spirit seemed to say to me. "You rushed ahead. You didn't wait in your spirit for My leadership."

6. According to Matt. 12:36-37, why is it important to have an inner attentiveness to God as we choose our words?

7. The Holy Spirit occasionally speaks in spectacular ways, but He does so only when it's necessary. More often He delights in guiding us in such behind-the-scenes ways that only in looking back do we realize that He led us. Can you recall times when you were not precisely sure what

God was saying but you went ahead, trusting that He was guiding you, and realized later how perfectly you were led?

If we are seeking to know God's direction and are unable to sense His guidance, we are to trust that God's inward voice has not left us but that He has nothing to say at this time. Even His silence we accept humbly and with faith.

God calls our faith "precious" in 2 Pet. 1:1. In fact, without faith it is impossible to please Him. See Heb. 11:6. Because our faith is of such great value to God, He often allows us to walk by faith rather than by sight. Know that when you are doing what you believe He wants you to do, even though the way seems unclear, He delights in your faith.

8. Why do you think our faith is so precious to God?

9. If we've prayed and trusted the Lord for guidance, then we should believe that He gives us a sanctified judgment. As we trust that He guides us, we can go forward believing we have the mind of Christ. Apply "According to your faith will it be done to you" (Matt. 9:29) to being able to trust Him to guide us continually.

10. If we've lost a sense of God's guidance in a certain situation, we should allow the Spirit to search our thoughts and conversation. What should be done if we discover we have been out of step with the Spirit?

11. The Spirit often guides by giving an inner hesitancy or a sense of rightness. How would a failure to respond to those inner nudgings of the Holy Spirit indicate a lack of faith?

It's not always easy to surrender our impulsive responses. However, when a remark comes to mind and we feel His check, we must choose not to say it. Silence may result, or He may replace our response with His response. As we allow the Holy Spirit to choose our words—or silences—He also will give us the attitude we should exhibit.

To abide (or "continue") in Christ is simply to abandon our self-life—to let go of every thought and desire of our own and look moment by moment to Jesus to form His thoughts and desires within us. Resting in Christ is a wonderful life of privilege and power.

Scriptural Role Model

When John and two of his disciples saw Jesus walking by, John said, "Look, the Lamb of God!" (John 1:36). How often we need someone else to help us be attentive to the Lord!

The men followed Jesus until Jesus turned to them and asked, "What do you want?" (John 1:38).

They asked a simple question: "Where are you staying?" (v. 38).

"Come . . . and you will see" (v. 39), He replied. They

went and saw where He was staying and spent that day with Him. It was as though He said, "Do you really want to know more about Me? Then come spend some time with Me, and I'll answer your questions."

What was the result of a day spent with Jesus? Andrew knew he had found the Messiah and went to tell his brother Peter. When we spend time with Jesus and learn more about Him, we, too, want to share with others what we've discovered and bring them into Jesus' presence.

Memorize

"This is what the Sovereign LORD, the Holy One of Israel, says: 'In repentance and rest is your salvation, in quietness and trust is your strength'" (Isa. 30:15).

Prayer

Dear Lord, give me ears with which to hear what You would say to me. I look to You to teach me. Show me Your ways, O Lord; teach me Your paths. That's what I want—Your ways and Your paths—not those of my own choosing. I realize how little I know about how to direct things. I want to learn to listen, to say only what You give me to say, to wait on You, to quiet myself in Your presence. Thank You for always being near, for always giving me what I need to say. In Jesus' name. Amen.

7

LEARNING TO REST IN A CRISIS

There may be no rest in outward circum-
stances, even as there was none in His, but
in our innermost being there will be a rest.[1]
                                —J. Gregory Mantle

Introduction

When our son, Gregg, and his wife discovered that a package of money they had shipped had been lost, his wife said she didn't panic. "We can pray that back," she thought, then reasoned that if God didn't return the money, He would provide in other ways because He had a better plan.

Resting is looking to God to take care of our situation and being at peace about it. His outcome may not be the result we think we want, but we rest in the knowledge that His choices are always best. God has arranged our highest interests and His highest glory to be the same thing.

"Take My yoke upon you . . . and you will find rest—relief, ease and refreshment and recreation and blessed quiet—for your souls," promised Jesus (Matt. 11:29, AMP.). To take His yoke is to submit to His will. Sometimes we learn to do this best in a crisis. "Trust is a journey where the biggest steps are taken when we're carrying the heaviest loads," our son wrote to us recently.

Discussion and Questions

In Matt. 26:38, when Jesus is overwhelmed He wants two things—to be near His closest friends and to pray to His Father. His friends failed Him, but God did not. It should be a source of strength to us to know that even without friends we can have enough grace from God to fulfill His will in our crises.

"Learn from me . . . and you will find rest for your souls" (Matt. 11:29). In the following meditation, let's learn from Jesus how to rest, the values of resting, and, finally, the results of resting in a crisis.

◆ How to Rest in a Crisis

1. *Jesus continued in prayer until He gained strength.* Jesus didn't pray just once. See Matt. 26:39-45. He prayed until He could leave the place of prayer with confidence that God was in control.

This is a crucial point, yet one we often overlook. How can we endure our trials with calmness unless we've gained that same confidence in God for our immediate situation? We often pray in a crisis, but fail to continue praying until we rely completely on God. What differences might such praying make in our response to the crisis?

2. *Jesus did not deny His human desires.* Jesus began His prayer by admitting His personal longing. See Matt. 26:39.

Rather than deny what we hope the outcome of our crisis will be, we should honestly express our fears and longings to the Lord. Why do you think is it important to recognize and tell God about personal desires?

3. *Jesus' deepest longing was for God's will.* Jesus next stated that His greatest desire was for God's will to be done. This step is necessary before we can rest in the knowledge that God is in control. What evidences do we see in the following passages that Jesus trusted His Father to be in control and to have the best plan?

 Matt. 26:37-42

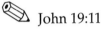 Matt. 26:53

 John 19:11

Notice that Pilate, desiring his agenda to be realized, could not do what he believed to be the right thing. See John 19:12.

How might a failure to want God's will above our own hinder us from being able to execute our good intentions?

Sometimes we're tempted to not surrender to God in a crisis because we fear He may will something we don't want. However, if we insist on our way and realize the momentary "good" we wanted, it may be a Pyrrhic victory. Pyrrhic was an Epirus king who fought a war against the Romans and won, but he used so many men that he couldn't fight again. It was a too-costly victory. When we win a Pyrrhic victory, our choice will not result, in the long run, in our highest good and in God's glory.

4. *Jesus did not depend upon human efforts.* See Matt. 26:50-52. Why does our rest often depend upon our seeing the futility of human efforts?

"How happy are those who know their need for God, for the kingdom of Heaven is theirs!" (Matt. 5:3, PHILLIPS). What will be evidences in our lives that we know our need for God?

5. *His focus was on truth rather than on personal desires to protect himself.* Notice Luke 23:27-31. It is difficult to maintain this focus in a crisis. What can we do to help us view a situation from God's perspective?

6. *Jesus did not defend himself.* In Matt. 27:12-14, we see that the governor recognized that this was highly unusual. What do you think enabled Jesus to remain quiet?

Jesus had an inner attentiveness so that He spoke only what the Spirit gave Him to say. Do you recall a time when you refrained from speaking because you felt to do so would have been disobeying God? How does such inner responsiveness give us rest?

Those who learn to trust the Spirit to guide their conversation find an increased ability to trust God to guide the outcome of the situation. Why would this be true?

Those at rest are not focused on what others are saying, but they are focused on obeying God. They do not need to respond automatically to all those who see things differently. God will defend them. What is the promise in Ps. 37:6?

Although Jesus was quick to defend His Father (as in Matt. 21:12), He did not react out of personal desire for revenge. Notice that in Matt. 5:39, Jesus said that when caustic words are spoken we're not to resist. How might resisting disturb our rest?

Learning to depend upon God is a continuing process. Recently a friend wrote:

> I woke up this morning with a scripture going over in my mind: 'My strength is made perfect in weakness.' It is a wonderfully soothing scripture. You know how refreshing a sunburn lotion is to your skin when it has been parched. I had that kind of cooling sensation over my spirit as God helped me claim that verse. I have been trying for the last three days to roll my burdens on the Lord. I believe this will do it. I am so weak in the circumstances we are in, but that is when God's strength is perfected.

◆ The Value of Resting in a Crisis

1. *Jesus understood the significance of His trial.* See Matt. 26:45, 54.

"The thing about real life is that important events don't announce themselves," Edith Schaeffer writes. "Trumpets don't blow, drums don't beat."[2] If we could hear drums impressively rolling in the background before our trials, we would likely trust God and rest in His faithfulness. All our trials are important, because our faith is precious to Him. How might we respond differently if we always understood the significance of our trials?

2. *Jesus was unafraid of others' actions, because He knew His Father was in control.* See Matt. 26:50-53. Believing that God is in control of all things is not saying that He causes such things as fires, floods, wars, or even AIDS (Acquired Immune Deficiency Syndrome). However, to say that God does not initiate our difficulties is not the same as saying that God does not speak through them or have perfect command of how they affect our lives.

Ronald Rolheiser writes that for his parents, who were farmers, there were no accidents. "If they had a good crop, God was blessing them! If they had a poor crop, well, they concluded that God wanted them to live on less for a while . . . and for a good reason! And they would always, in the deep parts of their minds and hearts, figure out that reason."[3]

Is it your habit to look at each event in your life and ask, "What is God saying to me?"

"His understanding no one can fathom" (Isa. 40:28). How true! Our minds cannot grasp the thought that His understanding allowed Him to plan the details of each person before the foundations of the world. How He could regulate such a system is unfathomable.

3. *Jesus did not react with irritation to His disciples' failure.* After time to pray was past, He didn't berate them for neglecting to pray, but simply said, "Rise, let us go!" (Matt. 26:46). He looked to the future rather than showing annoyance at past mistakes.

Why is it so hard to obey the words "Do not fret" (Ps. 37:1, 7, 8), when we are in a crisis?

Of what benefit is it for us to be able to take others' mistakes calmly?

If we are naturally quick and impetuous, we'll find that cultivating the habit of remaining calm is a great help toward gaining an inwardly even spirit.

One valuable way to maintain rest is to guard against grumbling. Many things can irritate us. An employee fulfills his task imperfectly, some order is wrongly obeyed, someone keeps us waiting unreasonably, people are forgetful or do their work carelessly. All these provide us with opportunities to have the mind of Christ. Try not to be disturbed. You may need to show the persons to blame where they are wrong, but avoid intense expressions of displeasure.

4. *Jesus saw that His willingness to obey was optional.* Notice in Matt. 26:53 that Jesus recognized that although He could avoid the suffering, God's will would not then be done. He chose suffering rather than His own human desires. If you are now confronted with a difficult situation, what choices can you make?

5. *Jesus had a different perspective than those who were reacting only to the immediate situation.* See Luke 23:28.

How does being calm in the midst of a crisis enable us to have discernment about long-range consequences?

6. *Jesus loved those causing His crisis.* See Luke 23:34, 43. Do you think He expects the same from us?

How can we tell if we love them? Consider 1 John 3:16.

◆ The Results of Resting in a Crisis

1. *Although Jesus trusted God, the situation did not get better immediately.* What were some of the discouraging events that occurred after He responded in obedience to God by not defending himself? See Matt. 27:15-31.

Often we're prone to think that because we're trusting God for the final outcome, the situation should immediately begin to improve.

2. *God was at work behind the scenes for Jesus.* See Matt. 27:32.

Those who rest in Him find evidences that God is providing for them even in the midst of their suffering. Can you recall glimpses of God at work even in the midst of pain? Often His love to us comes through other people, scriptures, even the beauty of nature. What recent evidences of His love have you seen while in the midst of a dark time?

3. *In the darkness, Jesus lost sight of God.* See Matt. 27:45-46.

Nothing brings our spirit lower than to have no sense of God's presence. Even we who rest in God will face dark moments when all we can do is say, "Lord, why? I've trusted and obeyed You. Why this?" An inability to see God does not necessarily mean we are out of His will. How does that thought provide encouragement?

4. *The people misunderstood Jesus.* When all He wanted was God, they thought He was calling for Elijah (Matt. 27:47). Have you felt misunderstood by others? How did you respond?

5. *Jesus was confident the final outcome would glorify God.* See Matt. 26:63.

It is one thing to see how God received glory from our past circumstances; it is often more difficult to believe He will be glorified through our present crises. Why is it important to believe that God allows only what can give Him glory, for those trusting Him?

6. *Jesus was not always complacent.* In John 18:23 and 34, what indicated that Jesus wasn't always passive? Why do you think Jesus asserted himself at this time, when He had remained silent earlier?

When Gregg and Sarah lost their package, their resting was not inconsistent with Gregg's going to the manager of the United Parcel System (UPS) office, reporting the missing parcel, and staying at the office until it was found. Why might complacency or passivity at times signal a failure to trust God?

Scriptural Role Model

Second Kings 4:8-37 provides a fascinating story of the Shunammite woman who was calm, but not complacent, in her crisis. Despite this woman's grief after her son died, she remained composed. Twice by faith she said, "It is well." See verses 23 and 26, KJV. She was not lying; she was trusting God. This mother expressed faith because she believed that God, through the prophet Elisha, would help her.

For us to be calm in the midst of a crisis we must know we're depending upon God. Have you ever prayed until you could say, "It is well," even though the answer was still unseen?

Memorize

"Come to me, all you who are weary and burdened, and I will give you rest. Take my yoke upon you and learn from me, for I am gentle and humble in heart, and you will find rest for your souls. For my yoke is easy and my burden is light" (Matt. 11:28-30).

Prayer

Dear Lord, You know I am facing a difficult circumstance. Please give me Your perspective and Your thoughts. Teach me to cast all my anxiety on You, because You care for me. What a reason to come to You! You care for me!

If I cast my care upon You, it is no longer my burden. Thank You for taking the weight of all my cares and letting me find rest in You. In Jesus' name. Amen.

8

IF WE AREN'T QUIETLY RESTING . . .

The faith that always thanks Him not for experiences, but for the promises on which it can rely, goes from strength to strength.[1]
—*Andrew Murray*

Introduction

Our faithful God enables us to discern why we lack rest. After we began *Women Alive!* magazine, I would go to the post office each day, eager to see what was in our mailbox. I began to notice that on the days many subscriptions arrived it was easier to rejoice than on the days when there were few. This bothered me. If I were really trusting the Lord, if this were His work and not mine, should it matter what came in the mail?

Late one night I was holding this matter before the Lord and asking that He search my desires. Would He help me to trust Him so my feelings didn't fluctuate with the mail? I wanted this to be *His* battle.

"Can you see that post office box as My hand?" He said. From that night, I could. In the months that followed, I could as easily give thanks for a few subscriptions as for many, by accepting the mail as from Him. How freeing it was to not worry but to calmly leave the results of our advertising with Him! I learned to rest in the knowledge that

He would provide. To remain at rest, however, I have to work diligently on the magazine. My rest depends upon an active faith.

Quietly resting is not synonymous with complacency. It is not nonchalantly hoping all will go well. It is vigorously doing all we can, while resting in the knowledge that God causes all things to work together for good to those who love and trust Him.

Discussion and Questions

Exodus 31:17 uses a bold term for Sabbath and describes God as refreshing himself (or "catching His breath") after six days of work.[2] God invites us to be refreshed as well.

We once had a minister who occasionally reminded us that the Israelites were to bear no burden on the Sabbath. What a relief that must have been to those people who had backbreaking loads to carry! Jesus has come to bring a Sabbath-rest to our souls—a relief from burden-bearing. To the weary He invites, "Cast all your cares on Me." See Heb. 4:9-10 and 1 Peter 5:7. If you have been unable to roll your load onto the Lord, perhaps the following suggestions will help you find refreshment in Him.

◆ We May Need to Care for Physical Needs

1. It could be that we are simply physically or emotionally exhausted. Elijah had "been very zealous for the LORD God Almighty" (1 Kings 19:10), yet he became so distressed he wanted to die. What things did he do before he was strengthened to go on? See 1 Kings 19:3-8.

2. Jesus' needs were ministered to by the angels. Even He was not expected to simply just pick up and keep going at all times. See Matt. 4:11. What do you think the angels provided for Jesus?

3. "Your Father knows what you need" (Matt. 6:8). "It is perfectly spiritual to sleep when your body demands it," writes Wesley Duewel.[3] We can find rest in the One who cares for all our needs—physical, emotional, spiritual. What kinds of needs was Jesus caring for in the following situations?

 Mark 6:31

 Mark 8:2-3

 Mark 14:6

 Luke 8:55

4. *Dear Father, I am trusting You to give me grace to work diligently when it's time to work, but also to give me freedom to relax when I'm tired. Don't allow Satan to convince me that You don't want me to enjoy physical and emotional rest. You are not a hard taskmaster. You know what I need. I feel that my physical*

needs include _____
_____.

*Please teach me to meet my needs in the ways You choose for me.
Thank You for saying, 'Come with me . . . and get some rest'
(Mark 6:31). In the name of Jesus, I come. Amen.*

◆ We May Not Be Resting in His Promises

5. In the Hebrew there is no special term for "promise." "Promise" is simply "word." God's Word is His
promise. With God no more is needed. He is so loving, so
powerful, so unchangeable that a word is enough. He
speaks, and it is done. Has God given you any words of
comfort or assurance? Those words will endure forever. Jesus said, "Till heaven and earth pass, one jot or one tittle
shall in no wise pass from the law, till all be fulfilled"
(Matt. 5:18, KJV).

Those who marched around Jericho dared, on the au-
thority of God's Word alone, to claim a promised victory
when there were no signs of this victory being accomplished. See Josh. 6:5, 20; and Heb. 11:30.

6. God often spoke to the prophets as if His promises
were already fulfilled. Rest comes when we are certain
God has heard our petition, and it's almost as though the
answer has come. In Josh. 6:2 and 8:1, notice that God
spoke in the past perfect tense.

7. God intends for His promises to be resting places
for us. When the Lord gives a verse, it's not just for that
moment. That word is good from that point on. "Your

word, O LORD, is eternal" (Ps. 119:89). Don't let go of the resting places the Lord gives you.

Ellen said that, when she was praying for some direction for her life as a college student, the Lord gave her Ruth 3:11—"And now, my daughter, don't be afraid. I will do for you all you ask." That verse not only gave her confidence that God would guide her then, but it has remained a resting place for her in the years since.

What promise has been a blessing to you, in which you have rested again and again?

8. When we share promises that we have discovered to be resting places for us, others are encouraged to find rest in those words also. For instance, an older friend said that when she was a young mother, the Lord gave her Moses' words in Deut. 1:17—"Bring me any case too hard for you." When her children's problems were too big for her, she took them to the Lord. After she mentioned this verse that the Lord used to encourage her faith, I too rested in that verse.

Recall and record some of the resting places the Lord has given others that have encouraged you.

"The love of the Spirit" (Rom. 15:30) breathes through all God's promises. Trust God to direct you to a promise in your regular reading, rather than skipping around trying to find the perfect verse. Read systematically, and He'll give you exactly what you need.

◆ We May Be Forgetting to Praise God

9. In Ps. 92, the psalm of the Sabbath, the Hebrews sang of God's love in the morning, and of His faithfulness at night (v. 2). This is appropriate for our Sabbath rest too. When we have a need, we can begin by focusing on His love—and after the situation praise Him for His faithfulness. God is delighted when we recall His works. See Ps. 105:5. Why do you think He is pleased with our remembering what He has done in the past?

10. According to Ps. 78:41-43, what vexed God?

Ruth Bell Graham tells of awakening at three o'clock in the morning with the name of one she dearly loved flashing through her mind. She knew there would be no more sleep for her that night. She lay there and prayed for that one who was trying hard to run from God. In the dark, her imagination ran wild.

Suddenly the Lord spoke to her: "Quit studying the problems, and start studying the promises."

She turned on the light, got out her Bible, and turned to Phil. 4:6-7. The *Amplified Bible* says, "Do not fret or have any anxiety about anything, but in every circumstance and in everything by prayer and petition [definite requests] with thanksgiving continue to make your wants known to God."

Suddenly she realized that the missing ingredient in her prayers had been "with thanksgiving," so she put down her Bible and began worshiping God for who and what He is and thanking Him for giving her the one she loved so dearly. She even thanked Him for the difficult spots that taught her so much.

And when she did, it "was as if someone turned on the lights in my mind and heart, and the little fears and worries that had been nibbling away in the darkness like mice and cockroaches hurriedly scuttled for cover."[4]

◆ We May Not Be Fully Obeying

11. Is it possible to rest in God and not demonstrate our faith through obedience? List three insights James gives about faith and works in James 2:17-24.

12. James says Abraham's faith and actions were working together, and his faith was made complete by what he did. We may believe God while praying, but to maintain the rest that faith gives, we must complete our faith through obedience. For instance, if you are praying for a child to be saved, what might be some things you could do to indicate that you are trusting and obeying God?

I sadly recall a day I tried to exercise faith without obedience. A friend called, saying, "I've just had surgery, and my pain is unbearable. Will you pray for me?"

She couldn't have called at a better time, I thought, remembering that I had decided to fast and pray that day. While praying, I thought of preparing our favorite casserole for her family. "All the ingredients are in the kitchen," the Lord reminded me.

"But, no, Lord. You've surely noticed that I've already decided to spend this day praying." Despite trying to earnestly pray, I didn't feel a sense of victory at the end of the day.

The next day my sick friend reported, "My husband was very unhappy about having to fix supper last night." What I had feared was true. I had not found rest in prayer because I had been inattentive to the prompting of the Holy Spirit. I had also failed to know His words in Isa. 58:6-7—"Is not this the kind of fasting I have chosen? . . . Is it not to share your food with the hungry?"

13. We cannot fully rest in God until we are fully obeying. It's interesting to observe some of the different acts of obedience God required in the Israelites' battles. In the following passage, what actions did God ask them to do to demonstrate their obedience?

 2 Chron. 20:15-17, 20-22

14. Notice their actions did not win the war. *God* gave them victory. But He would not act until they obeyed. This is an important concept. Often we fail to act because we can't see how our small efforts could accomplish God's work. But what is God's work, according to John 6:29?

◆ We May Need to Accept That an Unchanged Situation Brings Him Glory

15. Sometimes God permits weaknesses or difficulties to continue because they will give Him opportunity to display His strength. Why was Paul not given relief from his concern? See 2 Cor. 12:7.

16. Paul was not content to accept his weaknesses until after he repeatedly prayed. When God convinced Paul at a very deep level that He could do more through him if He did not remove Paul's "thorn in the flesh" (v. 7), Paul was at rest. See 2 Cor. 12:8-10. How did he state his contentment?

17. Do you find that some things are hard to accept as God's will for you? What if the Lord said to you, "I can remove the load you're carrying if that is what you want. But I will receive more glory if you carry it awhile longer"? What would be your answer?

◆ We May Be Hindered by Guilt of Past Failures

18. Satan tries to chip away at our faith, and one of his most frequently used tools is guilt. "You can't rest in the

Lord, because you haven't been faithful," he sneers, as he points to some area of failure. We see where he's pointing and conclude he must be right. So we give up our claim on the land of rest, drop our eyes from God's promises, and decide the life of abiding in Christ must be for those who are more faithful than we.

When this happens, we need to consider God's faithfulness to provide rest for the Israelites even when they had not been faithful.

In the following passages, how had the Israelites shown signs of disobedience and unbelief before the battle? Did God withhold His help?

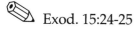 Exod. 14:10-14, 28

Exod. 15:24-25

19. Once we've confessed our area of failure, God is eager to help us. He is quick to forgive and to help in our immediate situation. The God who calls us to rest is also a God of mercy. When Satan tells us we cannot go forward because we've disobeyed, we can say with the psalmist, "The LORD has heard my cry for mercy; the LORD accepts my prayer" (Ps. 6:9).

20. Scriptures show God doing good to people who have gotten themselves into terrible trouble because of their own sins. The Lord is looking for people to bless who despair of themselves and look wholly to Him for the help they need. See Ps. 86:4-5.

Scriptural Role Model

We're tempted to think we're not worthy of God's help when we've failed, but God's love is amazing! In Josh.

7 and 8, He used the first defeat caused by disobedience to help the Israelites win their next victory. At first Joshua sent only 3,000 to fight against Ai, but because Achan had sinned, they lost this battle.

By this time, though, they knew that 5,000 men would not be enough to fight, so Joshua chose 35,000 men—all the people of war. Ai incorrectly assumed that Israel was again attacking with a small army, as they had earlier. This time the Israelites' victory was complete. Despite their previous defeat, the Lord gave them a permanent victory. They weren't ruined by failure.

Never despair. God can use past defeats to give you a total and lasting victory. Rest in the God who "delights in those" (Ps. 147:11) who "hope in his mercy" (v. 11, KJV).

Memorize

"Let the beloved of the LORD rest secure in him, for he shields him all day long, and the one the LORD loves rests between his shoulders" (Deut. 33:12).

Prayer

Dear Lord, You've invited me to taste and see that You are good. The rewards of obeying You are far greater than I can know before I obey. Teach me to persevere in obedience and to rest in the knowledge that You will richly supply all my needs in Your perfect timing. In Jesus' name. Amen.

APPENDIX

SUGGESTIONS FOR LEADERS

Prayerfully Prepare

If you have a desire to lead a Bible study, consider the desire to be a gift from God. "Delight yourself in the LORD and he will give you the desires of your heart" (Ps. 37:4). God never gives you a desire to do a task for Him without providing all you need to accomplish it. Your most important qualification for this role is a sense of dependence on the Lord for His perfect provisions.

Lorne Sanny said, "Prayer is the battle; witnessing is taking the spoils." It's just as true to say, "Prayer is the battle; leading a small group is taking the spoils." You lead with more confidence if you have prayed until you are trusting God to do His work in the group. Through prayer you gain a sensitivity to the Holy Spirit so you can allow Him to guide the discussion according to the needs of the group.

As you study, seek to find from the Word a truth that excites you. Your excitement for the Word will be contagious. The psalmist wrote, "Blessed is the man . . . who finds great delight in his commands" (Ps. 112:1). *The Living Bible* adds that such a person "shall have influence and honor" (v. 9).

If the truths you seek to share have reached only your intellect, they will likely reach only the intellect of those in your group also. But if the truths have reached your heart and changed your life, then there is a great chance they will reach the hearts of your group members and be life-changing for them as well.

Rely upon the Lord to be the Teacher, because spiritual truths must be taught by the Spirit. Isaiah 55:10 promises that the Word will be "seed to the sower, and bread to the eater" (KJV). Your role is simply to sow the seed. As you do, God promises to provide the miracle of turning it into bread for those who receive it. Before every group meeting, ask God to provide spiritual bread for each one coming.

In the Tabernacle, there was always to be "the bread of the Presence" on the table "at all times" (Exod. 25:30). As you trust Him, God will always provide the exact bread each one needs that day. When you are tempted to think your supply of seed is exhausted, claim 2 Cor. 9:10—"Now he who supplies seed to the sower and bread for food will also supply and increase your store of seed and will enlarge the harvest of your righteousness."

Lead with Confidence

Be willing to share how God has worked in your life. Paul asked that his listeners follow him as he followed Christ. "Whatever you have learned or received or heard from me, or seen in me—put it into practice" (Phil. 4:9). As you allow the group members to see how you follow Christ, you not only show them how to follow Him, but also you provide the motivation. Many times Christians know what they must do to follow Christ, but they simply need the leadership of one who is wholeheartedly committed to obedience. Be that person for those in your group.

Keeping the Bible study alive and friendly is imperative. Your own attitude is a key factor in the group's enthusiasm. Develop a genuine interest in each person's remarks, and expect to learn from each individual. Concentrate on developing acceptance and compassion in the group.

Don't be afraid of silence after asking a question. Give everyone time to think. Use "What do you think?" questions. These can help keep the discussion from seeming pressured or unnatural, since there is no such thing as a wrong answer to such a question.

Remember that your goal is not simply to lead an interesting discussion, but also to help group members understand and apply God's Word so it becomes life to them. "They are not just idle words for you—they are your life" (Deut. 32:47).

Occasionally suggest, "Next week let's bring to our group the verses that have especially ministered to us." Usually a verse becomes special when it meets a personal need, so group members will often share needs as well. Studying Scripture develops bonds of true friendship.

Remember Mal. 3:16 when enjoying the breaking of spiritual bread that occurs in group Bible studies: "Then those who feared the LORD talked with each other, and the LORD listened and heard. A scroll of remembrance was written in his presence concerning those who feared the LORD and honored his name." The Hebrew word for "listened" paints a picture of a mother bending over to listen to her children. Imagine God listening to you speak of Him and telling His recording angel to write your conversation in a journal in heaven!

"The lips of the righteous know what is fitting" (Prov. 10:32). Lead with confidence, because the Lord will help your words to be appropriate as you learn to depend on Him.

Practical Tips

"In his heart a man plans his course, but the LORD determines his steps" (Prov. 16:9). As you make plans to respond to the desires He has given, the Lord will direct your steps and provide the specific guidance needed.

Although these lessons assume that those who are studying are Christians, welcome all who wish to join you. In the Early Church, the Lord added to their number. He is still Lord of the harvest and knows whom to draw. He will give a desire to all those who should be a part of your group. Depend upon the Lord to direct those who would profit from the study to attend. Edith Schaeffer stated that the workers at L'Abri Fellowship—a Swiss chalet opened by Francis and Edith Schaeffer for young people with philosophical questions—asked God to bring those who should come there to study and to keep away those who should not.[1] (It will be difficult for a majority to participate in the discussion if the group is larger than 10 or 12.)

Unless you are meeting as a Sunday School class or other regularly scheduled meeting at church, the ideal setting would be the home of a hospitable member of the church. Trust the Lord for details regarding the time and place for weekly group meetings. Perhaps you could meet once when everyone can come, and then determine the details.

If you as the leader come early, you do more than set a good example. You also communicate your enthusiasm and delight in the group.

Begin on time, even if not all members are present. Be sure chairs are set up so that latecomers can easily join you. Don't ignore latecomers, but don't let them disrupt the session. Greet them warmly and then return to the study.

If you decide to include refreshments, a sheet can be available at the first meeting inviting those to sign who would like to provide refreshments.

Begin with prayer. Prayer is more than a transition from small talk to Bible study. You are providing the group with a consciousness that they are in God's presence.

Give time for prayer requests either before the opening or the closing prayer. If someone has a special need, ask for volunteers who will spend 5 or 10 minutes during the next week in prayer for that person. Twelve 5-minute periods of prayer equal an hour of prayer! Send around a sheet of paper with the prayer request written down, and ask group members to indicate how many minutes they will pray, to help them feel they have indeed committed themselves to prayer.

You may want to begin each session by reviewing memorized scripture. Encourage group members to write down either the suggested verse or a passage that challenges or encourages them and reflect on it during the next week. They will find it beginning to affect their motives and actions. We forget quickly what we read once, but we remember what we ponder and act upon.

A few of the questions will be most easily understood if the *New International Version* is used.

Rather than moving mechanically through the written questions in each lesson, you may want to prepare some of your own questions. Write them in advance and ask yourself if they are relevant and if the responses will teach what you think is important in this lesson. Avoid asking anything that is so personal the group members might find it threatening, unless you are willing to respond to the question first. As you share how God has convicted, encouraged, or instructed you through His Word, others will be drawn into sharing also.

End on time. If you say the study will be over at 9:00, end at 9:00. Then if any group members want to stay and visit, they can. This allows those with schedules to keep or children to pick up to exit without feeling that they are missing part of the study.

Keeping in contact between weekly meetings is important. Make group members' burdens your own and let them know that you are praying for them. When members are absent, call to tell them you missed them, but don't pressure them to attend.

You are "God's workmanship, created in Christ Jesus to do good works, which God prepared in advance for us to do" (Eph. 2:10). All you need for this study has been preplanned by Him.

Additional Chapter Comments

Chapter 1

God wanted the Israelites to understand that their Promised Land of rest would be a place where they would lack nothing. He invited them to walk through it and discover that one cluster of grapes required two of them to carry it (Num. 13:23). Yet because of their unbelief and disobedience they wandered for 40 years in the wilderness.

Our lack of rest is also caused by a failure to receive through faith and obedience all we can have in Christ. Through Him we can have an abundance and be fully satisfied. This chapter is to help us hunger for more of Him. "Therefore, while the promise of entering His rest still holds and is offered [today], let us be afraid [to distrust it]" (Heb. 4:1, AMP.).

Additional Notes:

Chapter 2

One of the great tragedies of the 1980s in Kansas City was the collapse of an overhead walkway in the fashionable Hyatt Regency hotel. More than 100 people were killed when the unsupported walkway crashed under the weight of people swaying to music and fell on those dancing beneath it.

After that catastrophe, one man reported that he had

stopped at a filling station on his way to the Hyatt Regency that evening. Annoyed with the slow attendant, he spoke some sharp words before driving away. He arrived at the hotel moments after the collapse. Humbled, he drove back to the filling station and thanked that attendant for saving his life.

How often we see our immediate situation and think we know what we want! We would quickly surrender our ideas if we could see the final outcome of some of our decisions.

The Israelites had no idea what the refusal to surrender to God's offer to enter the Promised Land would cost them. God wanted His people to realize what a wonderful land awaited them, so He said to Moses, "Send some men to explore the land of Canaan, which I am giving to the Israelites" (Num. 13:2). Twelve men went and came back with the report "It does flow with milk and honey!" (v. 27).

"But the people who live there are powerful, and the cities are fortified and very large" (v. 28), they continued. "We aren't able to take the land," they declared; and because they didn't believe God could give them such a land, they disobeyed Him by refusing to enter.

Their cost was great. "I will do to you the very things I heard you say: In this desert your bodies will fall. . . . Not one of you will enter the land I swore with uplifted hand to make your home" (Num. 14:28-30).

Sometimes the cost of surrender seems too high at the moment. However, we often realize later that not surrendering is even more costly. We can be certain that the rich young man in Matt. 19 always remembered that he chose not to surrender to Jesus. Ask the group to discuss how they think he might have felt about his decision when he was an old man. Also, how might he have benefited if he had yielded to Christ and sold all he had and given it to the poor?

Additional Notes:

Chapter 3

The Israelites found their rest in Canaan; we find our rest in Christ. All that Canaan pictured, Christ fully provides for us.

In this chapter we learn that to live in Christ is to live in love. When we move out of love, we move out of Christ. In fact, our ability to come into God's presence with confidence often flows out of our loving others "in action and in truth."

It may be important to point out, however, that we lack confidence because of our own shame rather than because God holds us off. God is often so much more ready to forgive us than we are ready to forgive ourselves. Discuss ways to regain our confidence in His presence, such as by confessing our lack of love and accepting His forgiveness.

Additional Notes:

Chapter 4

If we're trusting God to work in a situation, we're not trying to do His work ourselves. We're helped in this work of faith by remembering that faith is a rest; it's ceasing from trying to accomplish God's will through our efforts.

Rather than ceasing from our own works, we find it's easy to assume roles only God can do. We assign ourselves the role of being a personal Holy Spirit for others. We take on burdens that only God can carry, rather than casting our cares on Him. Hopefully by the end of this chapter the group will be more aware of ways they assume God's work rather than finding His rest.

You may want to direct the group members to think of areas in which they are most prone to push ahead in their own strength and then to identify their accompanying "work." "Anyone who enters God's rest also rests from his own work" (Heb. 4:10). "The promise of entering his rest still stands" (v. 1), but we frequently try to do His work instead of entering His rest.

Additional Notes:

Chapter 5

Jehoshaphat learned to rest in a crisis by taking the steps found in 2 Chron. 20. We can apply those principles to any area of unrest:

He faced the problem squarely.

He ceased all trust in the flesh.

He concentrated completely on God.

He continued in prayer until he heard from God.

He made a commitment to obey.

He collected the riches from the crisis.

Encourage those in your group to think of a present circumstance in light of these principles.

Additional Notes:

Chapter 6

Life in Christ is lived by attentiveness to the Holy Spirit. As we decide to "fix our eyes on Jesus" (Heb. 12:2), we discover ourselves being drawn into His presence. Our goal in being inwardly attentive is not a blanking out of our minds, but rather a refocusing of our thoughts.

The Quakers understand the need for ceasing their own activities to hear God. A vital part of their time together is spent in silence, each one quieting his or her own thoughts to become aware of what the Lord is saying within.

We were created with an awareness of the spiritual world and a need to be in contact with it. Many people, longing for the reality of communion with the Holy Spirit, seek spiritual realities elsewhere and are trapped in Eastern mystical religions.

Cultic spirit-to-spirit encounter is prevalent in our society. Satan is the great copycat. Mark Virkler points out that the presence of the counterfeit is proof that a real item exists. No one would make counterfeit $21 bills, because no one would want them. Also, no one will take the time to make counterfeit $1 bills. They are not worth the effort. Satan's counterfeit of spiritual encounter indicates that he considers true Holy Spirit encounter to be of great value.[2]

Be sure to relate the idea of inner attentiveness to quietly resting. How hard it is to rest in the Lord when our minds are not set on things above!

Additional Notes:

Chapter 7

"There is a place of quiet rest, . . . a place where all is joy and peace,"* a place where our greatest reality is our rest. "I will come to give rest to Israel," God promises (Jer. 31:2).

Ask the group why we often fail to experience this promised rest in a crisis. Is it because we don't know how to rest, or because we don't put forth the necessary effort? Do we simply not realize the glorious possibilities? Would we rest if we were certain that God provides rest for us in every rough place? "The LORD gave them rest on every side" (Josh. 21:44).

Do we cherish our wrong attitudes that prevent our resting? Do we not look to Jesus, but instead look to others who know nothing about resting?

*"Near to the Heart of God"

Additional Notes:

Chapter 8

Deuteronomy 28:65-67 presents a picture of the heart that is not at rest. It may help class members to gain a better view of the heart at rest to see it in light of the following graphic points from these verses.

The Israelites were told that if they did not carefully follow all the words of the Law, they would find no repose, no resting place. For instance, the Lord would give: "an anxious mind, eyes weary with longing, and a despairing heart" (v. 65). They would "live in constant suspense, filled with dread both night and day, never sure of [their lives]" (v. 66).

What similarities are there between this description and the lives of many people today?

Additional Notes:

Notes

Chapter 1

1. Hudson Taylor, *Hudson Taylor's Spiritual Secret* by Dr. and Mrs. Howard Taylor (Chicago: Moody Press, 1983), 179.

2. Ibid., 177.

Chapter 2

1. Amy Carmichael, *You Are My Hiding Place,* arranged by David Hazard (Minneapolis: Bethany House Publishers, 1991), 99.

2. H. D. M. Spence and Joseph S. Exell, ed., *Deuteronomy, The Pulpit Commentary* (Grand Rapids: Wm. B. Eerdmans Publishing Co., 1962), 3:107.

3. Carmichael, *You Are My Hiding Place,* 96.

Chapter 3

1. Andrew Murray, *God's Best Secrets,* Clarion Classics (Grand Rapids: Zondervan Publishing House, 1979), December 7.

2. Rosalind Goforth, *How I Know God Answers Prayer* (Grand Rapids: Zondervan Publishing House, 1921), 138.

Chapter 4

1. *I Promise You a Crown: A 40-Day Journey in the Company of Julian of Norwich,* ed. David Hazard (Minneapolis: Bethany House Publishers, 1995), 21.

Chapter 5

1. Ruth Bell Graham, *Prodigals and Those Who Love Them* (Colorado Springs: Focus on the Family Publishing, 1991), 40.

2. W. B. Godbey, *Deeper Things* (Louisville, Ky.: Pentecostal Publishing Company, n.d.), 74.

Chapter 6

1. Madame Jeanne Guyon, quoted in Richard Foster, *Prayer—Finding the Heart's True Home* (San Francisco: Harper San Francisco, 1992), 93.

2. Colleen Townsend Evans, *The Vine Life* (Lincoln, Va.: Chosen Books, 1980), 60.

3. William Law, *The Heart of True Spirituality, John Wesley's Own Choice* (Grand Rapids: Zondervan Publishing House, 1985), 1:40.

Chapter 7

1. J. Gregory Mantle, *Better Things* (Salem, Ohio: Convention Bookstore, n.d.), 80.

2. Edith Schaeffer, *L'Abri* (Wheaton, Ill.: Tyndale House Publishers, 1976), 53.

3. Ronald Rolheiser, *Against an Infinite Horizon* (London: Hodder and Stoughton, 1995), 167.

Chapter 8

1. Andrew Murray, *The Prayer Life* (Salem, Ohio: Schmul Publishers, n.d.), 53.

2. *The International Standard Bible Encyclopaedia*, ed. James Orr (Grand Rapids: Wm. B. Eerdmans Publishing Co., 1976), 4:2630.

3. Wesley L. Duewel, *Touch the World Through Prayer* (Grand Rapids: Zondervan Publishing House, 1986), 235.

4. Graham, *Prodigals and Those Who Love Them*, 39-40.

Appendix

1. Schaeffer, *L'Abri*, 124.

2. Mark Virkler, *Dialogue with God* (South Plainfield, N.J.: Bridge Publishing, 1986), 45.

OTHER BOOKS IN THE SATISFIED HEART SERIES

SIMPLY TRUSTING
083-411-6049

Simply Trusting will guide you in deepening your faith and living with the confidence that God will answer your prayers.

BOLDLY ASKING
083-411-6057

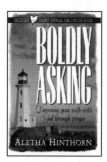

Discover what it means to come boldly to God in joyous praise, to bring requests, and to expect the abundance of life devoted to unhindered prayer.

JOYFULLY FOLLOWING
083-411-6065

Add depth to your Christian walk through the joy—and absolute necessity—of following the Lord in wholehearted obedience.